MINDSET MAGIC

Using Scientific & Spiritual Principles to Create Your Life

KRYSTI TURZNIK

Powerful Mind Publishing

For Arwen

*You were, have been, and always will be that magical spark that
ignites the deep yearning within me to search for deeper truth.
You are my inspiration, my love, and my joy.
For you I will be forever grateful. I love you.*

CONTENTS

ACKNOWLEDGMENTS

This book has been a labor of love. Along the way there have been people who have profoundly impacted me and helped bring this book to life. For them I am eternally grateful.

To my daughter, Arwen, you have been my soulful muse that started this journey. Thank you for the privilege of being your mom and watching you to grow into who you truly are. You have taught me more than you will ever know.

To my husband, Michael, thank you for being by my side and walking this journey with me. Life with you has helped me to ask the deeper questions of motivation and search for the invisible truth underlying every encounter. I hope you know how significantly you have shaped my life.

To my parents, Tom and Vickey, thank you for always being by my side. Your unconditional love and support has uplifted and carried me through the good times and the bad. You have given me the freedom to discover my truth. Thank you for teaching me I can do anything I set my mind to.

To my father, Phil, thank you for being my most difficult lesson in life. The distance I've traveled on the way to discover myself has been in part because of your influence. Thank you for being exactly what my soul needed.

To my friends, who have always been my cheerleaders, thank you for always encouraging me onward to bigger and better things. Thank you for being there and for always challenging me to reach even higher.

To my readers, to you, thank you for allowing me to be a part of your journey back to yourself. May what I offer touch the parts of you that need it in this moment.

To the Source of everything, thank you.

PREFACE

It was the middle of the night. All was quiet except for the sound of my breath and the whispers around us. We had talked for so long up until this point in our own special way. Now we traveled this last stretch together as we never would again. It was something between just the two of us, bound to deeply impact the course of our lives forever.

I felt the crown of her head. "Almost here," I thought. I gave my breath to her. A few moments later I held her on the outside rather than within. In my arms, I now held a beautiful, sacred spirit contained within a tiny newborn human body. I knew her from our intimate time together and she knew me, our bond innately pure and true. Yet somehow, I knew that she understood more than I at that moment.

As I looked down at her I couldn't comprehend how she came to be cradled in my arms. Surely it wasn't me; and it wasn't my husband who was sitting behind me either. Each of us wanted her so desperately yet we did not have the power alone to create and bring her forth. No, that magical power most certainly was something beyond us. And yet here she was, having come through me, so I must have played a part.

What part was it exactly? How is it possible that I could be a part of a beautiful creation and not understand? "I must understand," I thought, "even if it means understanding I will never fully understand."

Perhaps it is simply a matter of faith, trust, and surrender. I do not know. But I hope to. And so began my journey, this journey, to discovering at least a few of the age-old questions for myself. For her. Mainly for her; so that she can create a bountiful life of joy and happiness for herself and those to follow her. This is my prayer.

The time has come for me to seek.

May Grace grant me one small peek.

That I may live and breathe Divine.

And know I Am beyond all time.

Join me on this journey to self-discovery.

Every event is a beautiful opportunity to learn something about ourselves, the things that are important, and those that we are better off without. It is true that we may encounter stark realities we felt were better when hidden; but we soon discover that when light is shined on anything, the monsters we feared seem less frightening.

I've discovered that each of us has more strength within ourselves to overcome any obstacle than we realize... that we have more power to change our lives than the power we claim... and that we can soar higher than beyond our wildest dreams if we only believe. Trust that the tide will always turn... that there is always a silver lining... and that you are more magnificent than you give yourself credit for.

And so it is to you that I wish for all the blessings that come with creating a life only you can imagine. May you discover your own potential in all that you do, wherever you are in life. It is never too late to take time for yourself, and you are worth the time and attention. Be gentle with yourself, and may all your wishes come true. Welcome the magical moments eagerly awaiting you, no matter what disguise they may wear. Most importantly, may you unlock your potential and experience your possibilities!

Your journey has already begun.

Wishing you all the best,
Krysti

INTRODUCTION

Why Do We Struggle?

It all sounds so easy. Think the right thoughts and the world is at your feet. Think the wrong thoughts and you doom yourself to pain, misery, and suffering. But if it's all so easy, then why are so many of us, the majority actually, struggling in life?

Positive thoughts, uplifting affirmations, and good intentions have been tried by countless people. Yet most are still smack dab in the middle of the same life they've always been living without anything having changed. Or perhaps if anything, things have changed for the worse now that they perceive failure in themselves as well as this latest attempt at making a better life for themselves. Still, there are those who have found tremendous success with directing their thoughts to those things they want in life, so there must be some truth contained within these methods.

So why does it work for some people, but not all? Or perhaps these methods are working for everyone, and those experiencing the same old results are somehow unconsciously sabotaging their own success.

Perhaps there is some underlying secret in the power of the mind that once you become aware of it, will enable you to unlock your potential and create a life of your dreams.

Perhaps there is more to you than you can imagine.

Search any library or bookstore and you will quickly discover that there are countless numbers of self-help books available on the subjects of creating one's own destiny, shaping one's life, manifesting one's deepest desires, and so on.

An underlying thread found in many of these sources – the majority actually – is the unbreakable unity and connectedness of everything there is, everything there ever has been, and everything that ever will be. At the deepest place within yourself, you are a piece of the Greatness from which all is thought, created, and formed, and will surely return. Only the method of delivery and/or the methods to learn ways to tap into this Divine infallible source within us differ. As its goal, each of these works attempt to bring you closer to merging with your true nature and realizing the innate power you have within yourself.

Put away your self-judgment or criticism for a moment and let yourself receive the offering within this book. Experience this opportunity to discover something magical taking place that you are intimately involved in. Open yourself to the possibility that you could be grander and more powerful than you had believed.

Both science and spirituality indeed are working together to create the life you are living. Now is the time to become an active participant in your life. You are ready. The world that awaits you once you do is calling to you, just as you are calling for it.

CHAPTER 1 - YOUR THINKING

How Your Mind Works

You have been given one of the most amazing gifts in the world. The ability to choose what to think, what to feel, how to behave, and ultimately the freedom to become the person you wish to become. The power of your mind makes this happen.

Ralph Waldo Emerson once pondered, "What is the hardest task in the world?" To which he replied, "To think."

The critical determining factor in thinking, and thus ultimately in your satisfaction or dissatisfaction in life, is the particular type of thinking you are engaging in.

Your mind is designed to think. It is simply its nature to do so. Scientific research is suggesting you think an astounding 70,000 thoughts each day. Out of all those thoughts, however, only about ten percent are new thoughts and ideas. The remainder consists of unchanged variations of what you have thought the hours, days, months, and even years before.

Day after day, your mind churns over the same material which has long since been a part of your mental repertoire. At one point in your life the bulk of your repetitive thoughts were new and unique thoughts or ideas, derived either from yourself or offered to you by someone else who was influential in your life.

Many of the thoughts and ideas that were handed to you when you were young from important people in your life, also had those same thoughts and ideas handed to them from people that were influential in their own lives. From the moment you were born, even before, until you grew to about seven years old, you lacked the ability to filter out all of those thoughts and ideas that might not be in your best interest from those that will support, nurture, and help you grow into your full potential. Your mind acted like a sponge, absorbing all the new information being provided to it at an astounding rate.

As you entertained and acquired each new thought, it began to shape your perceptions about the world around you. You began to view the world as something which is either hostile, limited, and dangerous, or as something which is kind, loving, safe, and generous. Your perceptions about the universe you live in, and your place in it, then began to shape your beliefs. These opinions and convictions you hold help you to determine what is or is not possible for you in life and to help you find your place in the world. Your beliefs shape your feelings about yourself, those around you, and the world at large. Your thoughts and beliefs influence the actions you take in any given situation, thereby creating the specific outcomes you are experiencing. Your thoughts are the cause; your actions are the effect.

Ultimately it all comes down to mindset. Your experiences, your goals, your successes, your everything, is really determined by the mindset you hold. Your mindset is the ruling mental attitude and disposition that shapes how you will respond to or interpret a given situation. It has been said that 90% of our results come from our mindset.

The rational, analytical, creative, intelligent, thinking part of your mind is your conscious mind. Your internal dialogue, daydreams, willpower, and wishes arise from here. This is the part of your mind you like to think is ruling your life.

A more powerful force, however, residing in the background is the true authority. The master gatekeeper in your life is your subconscious mind. Herein lies the deep part of your mind that holds your core thoughts, feelings, and beliefs. Not the ones you would like to have, but those that you may or may not wish you had. Herein lies the naked truth you believe about yourself and for yourself.

As you go through life, every encounter and experience has the opportunity to teach you something new or reinforce a belief you hold. However, events by their nature are neutral. They just "are". They have no meaning except the meaning you assign to them. As an individual you can judge these events as something with either a positive or negative slant. How you judge these events depends upon your experience, perspective, and expectations. This is why the same event experienced by two different people with the same backgrounds can be perceived in two entirely different ways. It is your interpretations of your encounters that matters.

Regardless of the manner in which you are judging the things that you experience, be they positive or negative, these emotional states of consciousness unquestionably impact your perceived available choices by either limiting or expanding your possibilities. Your feelings then shape your behaviors and actions which in turn shape your experienced reality.

The world without, your external world, will always echo your world within, your inner state of being. It is your own personal hologram. The outer world of circumstances and experiences that you have will always intimately reflect the state of the inner mental world of your thoughts, feelings, and beliefs.

"Your thoughts, feelings, and visualized imagery are the organizing principles of your experience" says Dr. Joseph Murphy. "The world within is the only creative power. Everything you find in your world of expression has been created by you in the inner world of your mind, whether consciously or unconsciously."

You are the architect of your life.

The environment is in essence your extended body. The circumstances and situations occurring outside of your body, meaning the events, situations, and occurrences in your life, will always mirror your internal landscape. It cannot be any other way based upon the laws of the mind and the universe.

"Thus the invisible forces are ever working for man who is always "pulling the strings" himself, though he does not know it." Florence Scovel Shinn goes on to share in the 1925 classic *The Game of Life & How to Play It*, "Owing to the vibratory power of words, whatever man voices, he begins to attract."

Deep within your own mind there is a part of you that performs an amazingly complex task. This part of your mind, called the amygdala or reptilian brain, is a small one-inch long almond-shaped structure that is one of the oldest evolutionary parts of our consciousness. It is part of your subconscious mind.

This part of your limbic system rapidly processes the billions of environmental data stimuli surrounding you at every moment. It is intimately responsible for processing your fear and pleasure emotions, while it is also directly involved in the storage and organization of your memories.

This structure helps to determine your life experiences by filtering out the information that you have deemed irrelevant and unnecessary so that you may focus your attention and energy upon those things that you've identified as being relevant and important to you.

The different types of data sought out, received, and interpreted by the amygdala and other neurological systems, whether positive or negative, will have tremendously different impacts upon the physiology of your body and mind, and thus is inherently responsible for the overall experiences you have. As a direct result of the data received by your mind, an immediate response from your nervous system will occur causing biological hormones appropriate to your interpretation of the perceived environmental stimuli to be released. This influx of either sympathetic (fight-or-flight) or parasympathetic (relaxation) hormones will further impact your physical, mental, and emotional wellbeing. The critical factor in determining which of these autonomic nervous system responses is activated is dependent upon your interpretation, meaning your thoughts, about a given stimulus you encounter.

In addition, once your conscious mind accepts a thought or an idea, neurological connections in your brain are either created or activated. The more frequently you affirm and strongly believe in particular thoughts or ideas, the more deeply ingrained into your subconscious mind these become. Accordingly, consistent repetition of these thoughts and ideas solidify the neurological network kindling of such beliefs until it becomes a mentally hard-wired and automatic response.

The information received by the amygdala is then neurologically sent to the prefrontal cortex which is involved in analyzing information, planning, and introspection (assessing your thoughts and ideas, internal dialogue, and reflections about the situations and world around you).

Every morsel of the knowledge, understanding, and wisdom you have gained throughout your lifetime then comes together to help bring about the end result of the thought or idea you have accepted as true.

When you gain the insight of your internal dialogue and consciously direct your thoughts, attention, and focus, your awareness of the critical role you play in your life increases substantially.

During this introspection, you may then begin to realize the power you contain within yourself to tap into this life-directing force. The resulting experiences that you then aid in shaping can dramatically increase in quality, fulfillment, and an overall satisfaction that you experience in life. Sometimes this awareness can exponentially shift the positive results you experience as you take a more active role in crafting the specific outcomes of your life.

It is simply a law of the mind that will bring forth whatever it is that you may be affirming, be it beneficial or destructive. Regardless of the multitude of possibilities available to you at any given moment, at any given time, your mind does not concern itself with whether or not this thought or image is perceived as something that will help you or harm you. It merely acts upon the messages that it is given.

"Whatever you claim mentally and feel as true, your subconscious mind will accept and bring forth into your experience. All you have to do is get your subconscious mind to accept your idea. Once that happens, the law of your subconscious mind will bring forth the health, peace, and prosperity you desire. You give the command or decree, and your subconscious will faithfully reproduce the idea impressed upon it."

Dr. Joseph Murphy again tells us "The law of your mind is this: The reaction or response you get from your subconscious mind will be determined by the nature of the thought or idea you hold in your conscious mind."

The law does not judge appropriateness of content, value, or intention. It simply responds in kind matching your expectations. It will find those things that most closely mirror your state of mind. Conversely, those things that do not match your desires effectively collapse as possibilities available to you on a quantum level; thereby they no longer remain a viable option in the physical level of your reality.

In 1935 Edwin Schrödinger conducted a thought experiment that demonstrated all possibilities exist at the same time indefinitely, until an outside force such as observation or thought cause all outcomes to collapse into a single result. This collapse of potential outcomes significantly limits the possibilities available to you.

The laws of quantum mechanics and your subconscious mind are infinitely creative and crucial aspects of yourself and your world. Understanding them can lead you to greatness and a profound sense of personal satisfaction and well-being. An ignorance or unawareness of them can lead you to tremendous frustration, disappointment, and lack. Your ability to understand and harness this power within yourself and within your world may be one of the biggest keys to living a joyous and fulfilled life.

Ultimately the choice becomes yours once you have gained this knowledge. You can certainly allow yourself to succumb to unpleasant mental statements, thoughts, or ideas if you choose to. By doing so, however, your mind becomes filled with thoughts of negativity, sorrow, fear, lack, and dread. These limiting thoughts and beliefs will then be reinforced each and every time they are repeated, thus limiting and ultimately collapsing the alternatives of these ideas. Over time, your entire mentality can shift into one of lack, limitation, victimhood, and poverty. These unkempt and draining thoughts can keep you stuck in a mediocre pattern of life that may have been passed on for generations or that you may have unconsciously fallen into living, by not remaining vigilant and/or aware of your internal dialogue.

But there is an alternative. An alternative that will uplift you and provide guidance and direction so that you may achieve your smallest or grandest deepest desires. Positive thoughts, statements, intentions, ideas, and imagery infused with feeling provide a mental energetic course of action that will produce creativity, opportunity, abundance, happiness, joy, and fulfillment.

These thoughts can effectively help you to achieve your desires. As you positively sculpt your internal dialogue, you allow yourself to gain clarity about what it is that you truly want to have, to experience, to embrace, and ultimately to be. As you do so, you close off all possibilities to yourself that are not congruent with your newfound clarity in desires. Those things that are out of alignment disappear from your reality.

In the revered classic *As I Think*, James Allen tells us, "I cannot *directly* choose my circumstances, but I can, and do, choose my thoughts, and so indirectly, yet surely, shape my circumstances."

So your task, your challenge, is to make certain that the thoughts you choose to think are in your best interest. You must confirm that they are in alignment with the goals you set for yourself. You must ensure they are for your greatest good. Your thoughts must enable you to move in the direction you wish to proceed, rather than stifle your best 'self' that you can become.

Surely, if you are to become all that you can possibly become, your attention must focus inward. Perhaps one of your most important tasks then is to get clear intention within yourself. By doing so, you allow yourself the opportunity to choose those things that are important to you and what you desire for yourself. You can gain clarity about what you really want for yourself; what you want to have, what you want to be, and what you want to do and experience. Then, when you understand what you want, you can empower yourself even more fully by making the rules of your mind work for you.

Furthermore, these silent and powerful rules direct and impact the outcomes you experience. To the unaware, they wonder why things always seem to happen to them, why things never go their way, why they were dealt a bad hand. They fall into the victimhood that can so easily penetrate one's mind when they feel hopeless.

Yet by understanding the rules of the mind, and successfully applying them, you can claim ownership of your mind and your life and begin to co-create the things you desire. Additionally, these rules, which are not rules but rather laws as they cannot be broken, are operating with or without your knowledge. They operate unerringly.

Without fail, every thought or idea causes a physical reaction. Each thought you think will always produce a corresponding biochemical environment within your body that matches your originating thought. It is an immediate and predictable response. A positive thought will produce a specific type of physiology, as will a negative thought produce its own specific biological environment. The body follows the mind correspondingly. As a result, your body will function drastically different with a positive thought than with a negative one. Your thoughts become things. All thoughts precede the physical reality you experience.

Your mind can only hold one thought at a time. It is impossible to simultaneously hold opposing ideas at same time. A choice must be made. If you wish to create magic in your life and consciously achieve your goals, it becomes your responsibility to choose which thoughts you will think, knowing that both positive and negative thoughts and feelings cannot occur in the mind that the exact same time. This personal responsibility and ownership of thought requires you to be committed to creating the life you desire, rather than being content to reacting to the situations you encounter.

The Law of Expectancy logically follows this understanding. What you expect to experience will tend to be what you actually experience. The filtering process that takes place in the mind's reticular activating system as well as in the amygdala will filter out anything in your environment that doesn't meet or match that same expectation. Your awareness will then be of only those certain things in your surroundings that reinforce your expectation. The opposing possibilities will collapse all opportunities for something that is not in alignment with your belief. What you think about you bring about.

Henry Ford was demonstrating the effects of this law when he said, "Whether you think you can or think you can't, you're right. Whether you believe you can do a thing or not, you are right. If you think you can or think you can't, either way you are right. If you think you can or think you can't, you're probably right."

The Law of Concentrated Attention works in conjunction with the Law of Expectancy. It states that whatever you concentrate on tends to happen. Your thoughts, beliefs, and expectations become a self-fulfilling prophecy, for better or for worse, because you are concentrating on them. Your focus eliminates anything outside of your narrowed beam of attention.

Your conscious mind identifies information in your environment through your five senses, compares it to previous experiences that are similar in nature, and categorizes and analyzes it accordingly. Thus, you can choose your thoughts at will, be they either constructive or destructive.

On the other hand, your subconscious mind must accept all thoughts and images given to it as truth. It is unable to tell the difference between what is real vs what is imagined. It has veto power over conscious thoughts and desires if they are not in congruence. It is the ultimate authority. Thus, collapsing all other possible outcomes not supporting your chosen thoughts or images. Your subconscious mind is the radio tower that then sends these chosen thought forms into the universe without question.

The language of your subconscious mind is that of images and feelings. Your imagination holds tremendous power in the creation of your worldly experiences. With laser-like precision, the Law of Imagination states that when will and imagination are in conflict, imagination will always win. Your imagination is more powerful than any knowledge you may gain, and will override that which is contrary to it. In order to create congruence between the chosen thoughts and desires of your conscious mind and the mental imagery of the established beliefs and feelings within your subconscious mind, the power of your imagination can be utilized to facilitate a cohesiveness between them.

Once an idea or belief has been accepted by your subconscious mind, it will remain in place until another replaces it. Additionally, the longer the idea or belief remains, the more opposition there is to replacing it with a new idea.

With the Law of Reversed Effect comes the understanding that the harder you try to do something, the more difficult it becomes. The greater the conscious effort, the less the subconscious response you will experience. If you would like to fall asleep but don't believe you can, for example, the more difficult the act of falling asleep becomes. Less mental effort will produce greater results, especially when you would like to do something but think you are unable.

However, the Law of Repetition demonstrates that the more you do something, the better you become at it. By repeatedly thinking or doing something, the thought or act then becomes stronger. Additionally, each subsequent thought and resulting action creates less opposition to each successive opportunity. In this way, habits of thought, feelings, beliefs, and actions can be formed with repetition. To make your habits even stronger, the use of your imagination will amplify your results.

The language your mind uses comes from your senses of sight, sound, touch, taste, and smell, as well as thoughts and images; simply stated, from your direct experiences. Therefore, since your mind directly relies upon what it has experienced, your mind can only process things in the positive aspect. This is called the Law of Positive Information. Your mind does not have the capability to perceive negative information, something that it has not experienced. It does not understand when something is unwanted but will instead identify with the positive information you have given to it. For example, if you decide you don't want to eat the cookie, your mind interprets your desire as you do want to eat the cookie. It doesn't comprehend the negative and construes your instruction in the affirmative to eat the cookie, thus making the thoughts and images that you choose to think incredibly important.

While stronger emotions tend to triumph weaker thoughts and feelings due to the Law of Dominant Effect, your negative emotions are stronger in the short-term rather than your positive emotions. You must be very conscious of this Rule of Negative Effect because if the negative emotions are dwelled upon they may soon become the stronger emotion that dominates your thoughts.

Since your mind can hold only one thought at a time, it is essential that your negative thoughts and feelings be cancelled as soon as possible. The Law of Substitution requires that a new thought fill the void of your eliminated thought, or the empty space will be filled with the return of the negative thought. Your mind will tolerate no void and will seek to replace what is missing.

You must create deliberately. Any thought that is not in alignment with your full potential is not allowing you to live your complete authentic self, nor will it produce the outcomes that you seek.

The Laws of Association identified by Aristotle outline the ease of which your thoughts will manifest into your experience. Whenever you repeatedly respond to a particular stimulus in the presence of another, you will soon begin to associate one with the other. Things or events that occur close to each other in space or time tend to get linked together in the mind (Law of Contiguity), such as thunder and lightening. The more often two or more things or events are linked, the more powerful that association will be (Law of Frequency). If two things are similar, the thought of one will tend to trigger the thought of the other (Law of Similarity), as in the case of coffee and tea, or peanut butter and jelly. However, seeing or recalling something may also trigger the recollection of something completely opposite (Law of Contrast), such as thinking hot often makes you think of cold, or up makes you think of down. Whenever either stimulus is present, the other will be recalled. The more you can connect those things and events that will produce your ideal outcomes, the faster this linkage will help to bring about their fulfillment.

Life is a co-creative process. Your conscious thoughts and subconscious beliefs both occur internally. Your actions are informed and ruled by your subconscious mind and ultimately result in the external manifestation of the outcomes that match your originating thoughts and beliefs.

Life doesn't have to be a struggle or a disappointment that leaves you mentally drained, physically exhausted, and physically depleted. Rather it will be a compilation of all of your empowering or limiting thoughts, beliefs, expectations, and fears. Once you become aware of your inner world, you can use that knowledge to break through your barriers and finally stop your inner struggles. The possibilities of a more magnificent future then open up to you.

Remember, you are not a victim, but an active partner in the creative process of your life. Stop acting like a victim or waiting for someone to save you and start taking full personal responsibility. For everything; the good, the bad, and the ugly... because you have created it. The simple knowledge of this personal power is a beautiful thing.

There are no more excuses. It's a choice. It's always been a choice. Only now you have more knowledge. Your innate free-will allows you to choose which path you experience, positive or negative. It's your choice.

CHAPTER 2 - YOUR DEPTH

You Are Deeper Than Your Physical Body

There is a place within you that is still and silent. It is a place where the chatter and demands of the day cannot penetrate, but rather remains untouched, pure, and true. It is the silent witness inside of you that knows everything is unfolding in the most perfect way, with the most perfect timing. It reveals the perfection of you and your importance in the world.

It is the place inside that knows you are here in this life for a great purpose, with great gifts to share; knowing your presence on this earth will move life forward in a way that only you are capable of achieving. History will never be the same because you lived, because of the way in which you touched the lives of others. The simple fact that you live carries tremendous insight into your innate value and worth, and the sacred responsibility of fully living the life you are meant to live.

You came here, into this existence, knowing the Truth. The truth about who you are, where you come from, and what you are here to do. You lived it. You breathed it. You were it and it was you. This was your reality.

It is a truth that you have long since forgotten because little by little it has been buried inside. Slowly the truth of your authentic Self became a faint memory as you began to integrate into the world around you and were molded into an 'acceptable' member of family and society. This molding has shaped your voice in the world, for better or for worse.

From your earliest beginnings, you absorbed the values and traditions of your family and cultural groups. As you grew, you began to establish some sense of individual identity, but your place in the world was often shaped by the influences around you.

Your shaping was necessary. It served a purpose that helped to facilitate your growth and development. Yet you have grown and understood much since then.

Perhaps you are sensing the silent witness within as it whispers that you can release the self-imposed limitations and doubts you have accumulated. The inner calling that you may feel burning in your belly is patiently waiting for you to realize that you are more powerful than you ever imagined. Yet it knows that there is work to be done and time keeps moving forward, so it's time to get down to business of getting clear.

Thus your new task is to rediscover what you already know, but have just forgotten. If you are fortunate you may have had experiences of your authentic Self, but all too often those moments are few and far between. Ultimately, when you remember who you really are, and decide who you wish to be in this life, you will be able to choose your impact in the world. At that moment, you can begin to move out of the mayhem and start making magic. The beauty is that once you tap into it, you can unlock your potential and experience your possibilities.

But first you must eliminate the outdated and unwelcome burdens and untruths you hold, so that you may excavate your wisdom within. Everything you are seeking you already have within yourself. All the answers to your many questions can only be given by the one asking the questions. You know everything you need at this moment in time to return to wholeness and truth.

It may not be a quick and easy journey; after all, contemplate how long it took to arrive at this place and time. But in truth, it does not matter how long you've been travelling upon this path. At any time you choose, you can take a different road, make a U-turn, or even create a completely new path.

What does matter is that you have begun your journey back home. Back home to your deepest Self and Truth.

As T.S. Eliot shares, "We shall not cease from exploration. And the end of all our exploring will be to arrive where we started and know the place for the first time."

In that spirit of exploration and understanding, when you look inward you can discover that you are an amazingly complex being with innumerable layers.

Let us start first with the external layer of biology, the physical representation of who you are. This is the tangible expression you often associate as being who you are. Yet this vessel in which you reside has, without fail, followed the blueprint of your thoughts, experiences, and your particular DNA. The biochemistry that you have provided to it has created a certain physiology that has resulted in this external expression of yourself. The physical environment within your body can be modified, as can the outer expression of your biology. The energetic force field produced by your body merges, shapes, and impacts on some level everything you encounter.

Next there is the outer layer you show to the world, whether true or false. It is the mask that hides you in varying shades of shadow, and prevents a full and honest expression of your glory and a pure connection with those around you. Yet sometimes you willingly cast off the mask for a moment or a span of time and allow yourself to become exposed and vulnerable as you reveal the perfection of your perceived imperfections. The splendor of you is fully revealed in those fleeting moments.

Then there is the inner layer in which you communicate with yourself. It is the level of your conscious thoughts, feelings, and beliefs; the one in which you tell yourself what you wish to be true or why things are the way they are. Here also lies the layer of the truth of things you know to be true but are to resistant to own completely; again, forcing them to live in the shadow of denial and therefore disconnecting you from who you really are. This is the way in which we perceive the outer world and the stories we tell ourselves about it.

The layer of your subconscious then follows. This is the part of your mind that is responsible for your automatic unconscious biological processes, as well as houses all your memories and experiences, and your core thoughts, feelings, and beliefs. These truths you hold for yourself significantly impact your actions, physical bodily expression, and your external worldly experience and situation.

Lastly, your deepest layer also has infinite layers within itself; layers of energy and spirit. As we now know, the world itself is made of energy. Everything there is, the tangible and the intangible, is simply varying frequencies of energy that can never be created nor destroyed. There is a constant energy exchange between all things, a web of connectedness from which there can be no escape.

At your core, in this deepest level of pure energy lies your Divine consciousness. It is the essence of your most significant and sacred Self. You are the individual expression of the Great I Am, the source of all things. You are made in the same image and likeness of That which was before you, and are thereby endowed with the same qualities of that Creator.

When you let go of your perceptions of who you are, you open yourself to the fullness and pure potential that is within you. Very often you hold too tight onto the outcomes in your life and you limit the opportunity for your authentic self, your spirit, God, Creator, Source, and/or the Universe to come through. You don't mean to limit yourself, of course, but many times you can find that you've been unknowingly living in a consciousness of fear and limitation.

Yet deep within, a part of you perhaps knows that you are a spiritual being having a physical experience. You understand that you are made in the image and likeness of The Divine and your essence is pure love, joy, wisdom, happiness, abundance, and all of the qualities of that great Source.

You are a spiritual being having a physical experience called Life.

Einstein's Theory of Relativity produced his famous formula $E=mc^2$ (e=energy, m=mass, c=speed of light) which indicates that all matter is simply an energy field. At your deepest physical level, you are particles of energy. Your body is a physical perception of energy resonating at a slow frequency. You are energy. Your observable universe is a reflection of the multi-dimensional layers of existence that are taking place in the unseen.

You are made from the same stuff that made the stars and galaxies. You are the breath of the universe. You are the creation. You are the creator. You are consciousness. You are awareness. You are love. You are beauty. You are inspiration. You are joy and happiness. You are the stillness. You are the truth. You are spirit. You are Divine. You are life. You are a seed of the Great I Am.

Thirteenth century poet and mystic Jalaluddin Rumi tells us "You are not a drop in the ocean. You are the entire ocean in a drop."

The apple that falls from the tree is endowed within itself the seeds of a thousand forests of apple trees. There is nothing the apple must do in order for this to be bestowed upon it. It simply is the truth of the apple. Each seed contains within itself the exact wisdom for the perfect unfolding of the apple seed to reach its full potential.

You are the intelligence of the Universe that is ever growing, expanding, and evolving. The inner desire, yearning, or restlessness burning within is your spirit within calling to shed the bonds of limitation, stagnation, and decay so that you can bloom into the dimension of your innate possibilities.

Living your fullest potential is what the Universe, God, Source, Nature intended for you. All of nature looks for expansion and growth. An acorn grows into a mighty oak tree. Within you lies that same great potential to grow into your full authentic self.

Yet the full expression of your complete authentic self will be vastly different than the full expression of your family and friends. You contain the blueprint within you of how to fully realize the gifts and greatness of *you*, and only you. You can be none other than who it is that you were born to be. Trying to mold yourself in to someone you are not is akin to the oak tree producing apples.

Your grand responsibility is to unfold into the being that you were born to become, thereby enabling the Universe to expand and evolve in a way that only you can make possible.

Fully embrace who you are at the core level so that you may cast down any lesser seeds of truth, where they will fall upon an impermeable barren landscape. Thwart the needs of any inferior seeds of thought so that they shrivel and die with the unfulfilled promise of what they could have been; something less than who you are meant to be.

Our current level of scientific understanding has yet to fully comprehend the vastness of the human spirit. Yet the spiritual teachings of the world, regardless of the particular dogma and rituals present in the individual religions, all have at their philosophical core this same wisdom that we are all able to rise up out of our suffering to behold something better. Throughout history every religion has told us that in order to do so we must take the right action that will enable this salvation.

Do not allow the truth of who you are and what you are capable of to get muddled from the voices on the outside. The world needs you now; not when you are ready, not when it's convenient, not when you everything is perfect, but now in this very moment. The moment your seeds of thought are buried into the rich substance that will nurture their fulfillment, underlying forces go to work to produce their ultimate expression. Your life, and everything you experience in it, all have their roots from within.

There is only one Mind in which you live, move, and have your being. Your thought and spoken words have power in them, and your every thought is a prayer, acting like a radio tower broadcasting your mental station or the gardener planting your seeds of tomorrow. Your subconscious mind is the intermediary between you and Infinite Intelligence; the womb where your thoughts are nurtured into their full potential. Form is the direct result of the union of thought and Source made manifest into physical reality.

The Universe hears every whisper of thought and immediately goes to work acting upon its fulfillment. The energetic vibration that you are emitting will draw unto you what you are thinking, as your thoughts become things.

Your direct relationship with the Divine Intelligence that permeates everything that is, was, and ever will be, is infallible.

"There is a thinking stuff from which all things are made," Wallace Wattles tells us, "and which, in its original state, permeates, penetrates, and fills the interspaces of the universe. A thought in this substance produces the thing that is imaged by the thought. Man can form things in his thought, and by impressing his thought upon formless substance can cause the thing he thinks about to be created. In order to do this, man must pass from the competitive to the creative mind; otherwise he cannot be in harmony with the Formless Intelligence, which is always creative and never competitive in spirit. Man may come into full harmony with the Formless Substance by entertaining a lively and sincere gratitude for the blessings it bestows upon him. Gratitude unifies the mind of man with the intelligence of Substance, so that man's thoughts are received by the Formless. Man can remain upon the creative plane only by uniting himself with the Formless Intelligence through a deep and continuous feeling of gratitude. Man must form a clear and definite mental image of the things he wishes to have, to do, or to become; and he must hold this mental image in his thoughts, while being deeply grateful to the Supreme that all his desires are granted to him. "

Your job is to think the best thoughts and allow science and spirituality to go to work for you. Consciously think your desired thoughts with deep feeling and let the Universe respond. Your thought seed is planted in the inner world and realized in the outer world of physicality.

When faith is combined with thought, the subconscious mind picks up on the energetic frequency, transmits it to the Infinite energetic realm of all possibilities. Faith is a state of mind which may be created or induced into the subconscious mind through repetition of thoughts and images infused with feeling. All thoughts that are infused with feeling begin to translate themselves into their physical equivalent immediately. It does not matter if the thought is truthful or fiction, harmful or beneficial. If repeated often enough and with feeling, a lie will be believed just as readily as the truth. In fact, the feeling added to any thought is what gives that thought its vitality and strength. Any thought or idea repeatedly spoken to the subconscious mind that is void of any associated feeling will have no impact. Blandly repeating affirmations or mantras will find no purchase on the attainment of your desires because they are not resonating within your subconscious mind. Those thoughts magnetized with the infusion of feeling draws onto itself that which is similar.

The Science of Mind states "Every time we think, we are thinking into a receptive, plastic Substance, which receives the impress of our thoughts. When we stop to realize how subtle thoughts are, how unconsciously we think negation, how easy it is to get down and out, we will see that each is perpetuating his own condition. This is why people go from bad to worse, or from success to greater success."

Every "I am" is a choice. You decide how you define yourself. The words you choose and repeat to yourself define you and either limit or expand the possibilities available to you in any given moment. The Universe operates in complete perfection and all is as it should be.

Yet it is an exercise in trust. Form your thoughts and impregnate them with feeling as you release it to the Universe. Trust that you've planted your desire and that it has been received and accepted. Hold the belief that the Universe is rearranging Itself in order to bring your desires to you, for your best and highest good. Your responsibility then becomes to ask, hold faith in its arrival, look for signs, and ultimately receive the physical macro-expression of your thought.

CHAPTER 3 - YOUR POSSIBILITIES

The Underlying Principles of the Universe

Out of the plethora of possibilities given to you at each and every moment in time, if you are to have any input into the course of your life you must begin to consciously select those thoughts and choices which will align you toward the achievement of your desired results. Your clarity of thought will help to propel you forward. Conversely, your mental murkiness or fogginess will slow or impede your progress. You can then become your own worst enemy.

"Into my hands are placed the exact results of my own thoughts; I receive that which I earn; no more, no less." James Allen continues to remind you of your power.

By first becoming aware of how you are directing your mind, of what you are saying to yourself via your internal dialog, you are able to identify those things you may or may not need to modify. Understanding and restructuring your thought patterns will then allow you to create the kind of life you seek through the consistent laws of the mind and quantum mechanics.

Claude Bristol once beautifully described in *The Magic of Believing*, the similarities between the thoughts you think and seeds planted in a garden. "Once the soil is prepared and the tiny seeds are placed in it, it is but a short time when they put forth roots and sprouts begin to appear. The moment they start upward through the soil in search of light, sunshine, and moisture, obstacles mean nothing to them. They will push aside small stones or bits of wood, and if they can't do that, they'll extend themselves and grow around them. They are determined to emerge from the ground. They blossom and give forth fruit, vegetables, or flowers, and they succeed unless some greater force destroys them. When we are not aware of the details of nature's secrets, we observe the seed buried for a long time in the dark gradually expanding and exerting itself until it becomes a thing of beauty or usefulness. Cultivate it, attend it, give it sunshine and water, and it grows into full life. Remember it always produces after its kind... Plant the right kind of seed... and habitually feed it with strong affirmative thought always directed toward the same end, and it will grow into a mighty force, finding ways and means of overcoming all obstacles."

So many times, we try to fix or manipulate our external reality. We believe the causes lie in other people or circumstances. We find ourselves in situations where an underlying theme in our lives seems to occur over and over. This theme will appear repeatedly in various forms until you eventually realize that you must be playing a critical role in the situations you are experiencing. That you must be planting the seeds of fruit you do not wish to harvest. It becomes an endless self-fulfilling prophecy of frustration and disappointment unless you awaken to the fact that you need to make a change within yourself if you are dissatisfied with the results you are experiencing.

It is only once you realize that your external reality is an exact reflection of your internal reality that you may consciously begin to reclaim your power. Remember, the external experience is a hologram of your internal landscape.

If you are unhappy with your outer reality, you must begin to change yourself from within. You must change your thoughts, your feelings, and your actions so that you may be transformed by the renewing of your mind. The Book of Romans 12:2 of the King James version of the Holy Bible tells you this as well.

One of the most famous versus from the ancient Vedic text known as the Brihadaranyaka Upanishad IV:4-5 is, "You are what your deep, driving desire is. As your desire is, so is your will. As your will is, so is your deed. As your deed is, so is your destiny."

Over and over throughout time and culture the truth of your power and abilities has been offered for you to claim and pursue.

Your inner world of thought is the microcosm to the macrocosm outer world of your circumstances and reality. This wisdom has been espoused for millennia and is just as valid and relevant today as it was for the ancestors of our past.

The Universal Laws of spirit, laws of nature, laws of quantum physics are absolute and unchangeable. Law is as It is. Law is law. There are no flaws. It can be no other way. Although man appears finite and limited, the law through which man works is infinite. There is no limit to the law, only limitations in man's understanding. It is law and law does not care if it is used positively or negatively, correctly or incorrectly.

You do not have to be able to understand it for it to

operate or exist. Many things in the world, such as electricity, are utilized efficiently without a comprehensive understanding of the way it works.

However, once you understand the laws you can consciously use them for a definite purpose. *The Science of Mind* says "Hidden away in the inner nature of the real man is the Law of his life, and some day he will discover it and consciously make use of it. He will heal himself, make himself happy and prosperous, and will live in an entirely different world; for he will have discovered that Life is from within and not from without."

Therefore, you benefit greatly by becoming familiar with several of the underlying laws and principles that are ruling your experience, regardless of your conscious participation.

Your world is not one of chance, randomness, and chaos but instead it is filled with order, perfection, and predictability. It is true that the outer appearances may appear to be filled with the former, but at the deepest levels of existence where the subtleties reside, truly the latter reigns.

At its most simplistic level, the universal law states that when you ask for something, it is always given. Always.

To start the process, you must ask with clarity and specificity. Failure to do so will surely result in disappointment with the appearance of your mediocre results, or perhaps even an uncertainty of whether or not they have actually appeared because your asking lacked enough details to properly identify their arrival.

You must first ask, then believe and await its coming. You must train your mind to live in one of positive expectation regardless of what you see in front of you. It is simply wishful thinking if you ask for something but don't truly believe that it can be yours. Hoping doesn't equate to expectation; they are different energetic vibrations. Hoping for something always includes a level of doubt that something will occur. A level of certainty, faith, and trust in the workings of the world are what is necessary to enable the manifestation of your desires.

Then you must act on opportunities presented, as well as any inner guidance and/or nudgings you receive. Sometimes even your setbacks become the setup for your desires to appear.

Law is the servant of your thoughts. Thoughts must and do manifest in direct relationship with the intensity and focus of your thoughts. Repetition of your chosen thoughts is required to imprint upon your subconscious mind where the greater laws of the universe can go to work to bring about its creation. These laws are perfect, infinite, and there are no failures in the universe.

You wouldn't have a vision, a desire, a dream for something greater, if it wasn't possible to achieve it. There is always a way. The simple fact that you have this idea means that it is possible. The Law of Polarity, also called the Law of Opposites, states that if you have a need or a vision, its opposite already exists for its fulfillment. Your clarity of thought, desires, and intention are absolutely necessary, and you must be deliberate. The Universe is looking for your command and conviction. The Universe cannot bring to you something if you lack that clarity or if you keep changing your thoughts. You are what you think about, and you receive what you think about. Thought are most definitely things.

In *Ask and It Is Given*, Abraham-Hicks tells us that with only a few seconds of focused attention, you can begin to activate the Law of Attraction and begin to experience manifestations matching that thought within a short period of time. When you hold your desire for 17 seconds of pure thought, the Law of Attraction begins to respond. It stimulates another thought that matches that same vibration and it joins that original thought, making it clearer and more powerful. Add another 17 seconds and it compounds the strength of that vibration. In as little as 68 seconds of focused thought, the universe will move enough so that you can begin to witness changes within and without. "When you repeatedly return to a pure thought, maintaining it for at least 68 seconds, in a short period of time... that thought becomes a dominant thought. And once you achieve a dominant thought, you will experience matching manifestations until you change it." The law responds to your thought, not your current state of reality.

The Law of Reflection that states that in your thought is the cause that reflects the effect. Your mental image reflects itself into the physical form.

What you put out into the universe through thoughts, feelings, and emotions, you receive back in direct proportion. The Law of Cause and Effect, also known as the Law of Karma or the Law of Action and Reaction, states that for every action there is an equal and opposite reaction. You reap what you sow. What you give to others, you give to yourself. What you withhold from others, you withhold from yourself as well. Your actions of thought produce the external reaction in the outer world. Cause and effect are but two sides of the same coin.

In order for you to get to where you want to go, the Law of Unfoldment states that you can only advance from where you are, to where you want to be, when you allow yourself to do so. You must allow yourself to shift your thoughts and beliefs into those that will allow that unfolding; those that support with great clarity the expression of that desire. You must open yourself to becoming more and greater than you are in this moment, trusting that as you do the world will unfold with its equivalent.

Yet the Law of Gestation tells you that there is an expanse of time that is needed for the Universe to create the object of your desire, rearrange itself, and bring the fulfillment of it to you. In the linear world of time, the receipt of your desires tends to not be instantaneous. This may be a blessing in that it allows you the opportunity to confirm to yourself and the Universe that your dominant thoughts are your desires. It is during this time delay after your asking in which you must continue to believe, expecting its arrival, and allow its entrance once it appears.

All things in the universe are continuously flowing in circulation at an ever-expanding rate. There is never lack. The Law of Circulation reveals that energy given in one area may return to you through another channel. It does not need to be given and received from the same source. Yet it will return to you in equal proportion of what was given.

However, when the flow of energy is blocked through thoughts of limitation, there is stagnation. You no longer become a conduit for the flow of giving and receiving, but are in fact the cause for your own deficiencies.

The Law of Resistance demonstrates that what you resist, persists. If you are resisting something and your thoughts and attention continue to be directed upon the thing you don't want, your energy has no choice but to flow toward your resistance. Your energy flows to where your attention grows. The thing you are resisting will persist as long as the self-imposed cycle continues.

Ultimately, any resistance is fear, but fears are not real. *A Course in Miracles* tells us that "Fear is not of the present, but only of the past and future, which do not exist. There is no fear in the present when each instant stands clear and separated from the past, without its shadow reaching out into the future. Each instant is a clean, untarnished birth... And the present extends forever. It is so beautiful and so clean and free of guilt that nothing but happiness is there. No darkness is remembered, and immortality and joy are now."

This moment is the only moment that exists. All is well in this very moment. Fear is a trick of the mind to keep you where you are. Stuck in the safe and known. Witness the fear while taking faithful action toward your desires. Give more energy and thought to your dreams than to your fears. Make your decisions based on faith not fear. When you align yourself with the flow of energy, you enable the abundance and manifestation of your desires to come to fruition.

Nature functions best with that which is the simplest and easiest. The Law of Least Effort tells you that you don't need to struggle or push so hard to accomplish your desires. They will arrive more swiftly when there is no resistance but rather an effortless ease. Adopting an attitude of peace and calm will enable you to focus on asking for and receiving the perfect expression of your desires.

After all, the Universe is continuously expanding and growing. Therefore, there are infinite possibilities and infinite abundance available to you at all times, as the Law of Plenty and the Law of Abundance state. As an ever-present source of creation, the Universe will always rise up to meet the demands asked of It. It is irrelevant if you observe someone with something you wish for yourself. In this world of riches and abundance, a bounty of goodness and plenty awaits you. You must only ask for it.

Yet all three levels of your environment, your physical surroundings, the people you spend time with, and your mental environment, must all support your goals and growth. So powerful is your environment, that the Law of Association reveals your success is often directly proportionate to the expectations of those around you. The presence of any negativity, fear, lack, or doubt must be outweighed with a 1:5 ratio of positivity, courage, trust, faith, and abundance.

Bruce Lipton, author of *The Biology of Belief*, states "Our thoughts are not contained inside our head. When we have a negative thought, it's not just a negative thought bouncing around in our head. It's a broadcast. In the world of quantum physics, it's an impulse that will return a similar response... What's the relevance? There could be ten people out there – nine in a positive state of mind, one in a negative. If we send out a negative broadcast, who is going to pick it up? Not the nine positive people – they aren't tuned to that frequency. Who is going to pick it up is the negative person. What happens if we activate a negative person with our negative broadcast? We bring them into our life!"

The potential richness and grandeur of the Universe is amplified through the Law of Fellowship which states that when two or more of similar thoughts and vibration are gathered for the same purpose, the combined energy directed toward your achievement is doubled, tripled, quadrupled, or more. This applies to the individuals you choose to spend your time with, as well as the joining of your minds.

"For when two or three are gathered in my name, I am there in the midst of them", states Matthew 18:20 of the Holy Bible. As above, so below, when your conscious and subconscious minds are focused on the same outcome, Divine Intelligence is there also amongst them.

There is a price you pay for each of your thoughts, whether or not you realize it. Law is impersonal and exact. It is bound by Its very nature to return to you the reflection of your thoughts. Your thoughts are mirrored back to you in kind, regardless of your understanding of how the Laws of the Mind and Universe operate. You plant the seed of a thought image, and the corresponding form is manifested in your world. There is nothing that can or will be denied to you when you impress the proper thought and feeling into the Universal Mind, as long as there is nothing within that is preventing its expression.

CHAPTER 4 - YOUR POTENTIAL

How far can you dream?

We all have the same potential within ourselves. You are created from the same indescribable "stuff" permeating every aspect of your universe. That same force that created the stars and the heavens also created you.

You are formed of stardust, and light, and an ever-expanding urge to move beyond the here and now by charting new territories into the realms where unknown possibilities and creation lie dormant. Being that your sublime constitution is transcendental in nature, you are inherently free of the earthly bounds that constrict you in what may be conceivable.

Yet you do not know yourself as this. Millennia of years of evolution have exposed you to a world of limitations and bounds. The struggles, setbacks, and resistance experienced as life crawled its way out of the primordial soup has embedded itself into that same life. You have forgotten that you simply "are" and "can be". You have forgotten that at any moment you can make a quantum leap to the next level and bypass the distance required to get there. But it requires a different level of thinking and being. It requires a level of inner attention that in itself can often cause more of the struggles, setbacks, and resistance you are trying to avoid. Yet the full expansion of your true potential can only be realized with that attention.

Metaphorically and literally you are eternal. Your reach spans across boundless time and space and into the eons of ages yet to come. The significance of your choices is such that they will alter the course of history. You are profoundly vital to the evolution of the world and yet you may not believe it. Miracles and magic are available to you now, in this very moment. As it has been spoken, you are not a drop in the ocean but the ocean in a drop.

Unfortunately, many times in life you can find yourself caught up in negative thoughts and limiting beliefs that do not serve the highest and best good of you and of those around you as well. Perhaps at one point in your life these thoughts were of value and served a purpose, but often they linger well beyond their usefulness. Perhaps you have forgotten that you are the ocean. You consciously understand that you no longer receive the benefits from the negative thoughts and beliefs, yet you continue to utilize these same tired methods to achieve your goals and create the kind of life you seek.

It is imperative you understand that you will continue to struggle unless you can make a shift. It's guaranteed.

You must be willing to make a shift in what you will and will not accept in your life. A shift in your own thinking. A shift in your expectations. A shift in your beliefs about your-self, your goals, and how to achieve them.

By becoming the best you can possibly become, by

making yourself happy and fulfilled, you will ultimately be contributing wonderfully remarkable things to the communities you live in and to the world at large.

You do so, of course, by becoming aware of your internal dialogue as well as how you feel under the influence of that internal self-talk, and consciously direct it to achieve your intimate desires. Also by remembering who you are and what you are made of.

Just like anything else in this world, your mind needs attention and maintenance in order to perform at its full potential. If you fail to create this awareness, you are ultimately holding yourself back from truly living your life to the fullest.

Regrettably, it is easy to let unkempt thoughts run rampant. It is those limiting thoughts that are filled with negativity, and sorrow, and dread that keep you stuck in the pattern of life that you've always been living, or perhaps have fallen into living, by not remaining vigilant and/or aware of your internal dialogue.

But to think properly and effectively in order to achieve the results you desire is often the difficult part. You are challenged to always strive for inner awareness so that you may gain clarity about what it is that you truly want to have, to do, to experience, to embrace, and to be.

Yet there is nobody who can do this for you. You, yourself, must be the one who claims responsibility for the outcomes of your life. Not just some of it. All of it. Your voice is the first you hear when you awake in the morning, and yours is the last voice you hear when you fall asleep at night. You are alone inside your mind with your thoughts. There is nobody else who can hear your deepest and most secret ideas and beliefs. There is nobody who is standing guard for you, protecting your mind from harmful or hurtful thoughts or ideas. You must become your own gate keeper and warden for that which is most precious and most powerful, and allow only worthy and deserving thoughts to pass through. You must challenge those that are incongruent with your deepest desires so that you may capture a magnificent future.

Once you allow yourself to open your eyes to your self-imposed limitations and blocks, the details of how you have negatively impacted the course of your life becomes crystal clear. It is at that point where you may begin to take an active role in shaping your life and ultimately create a life of your dreams. Once you truly develop a cooperative and nurturing relationship with your inner-self, it is likely to lead you to healthier and more fulfilling life.

At the heart of it, the secret is to become aware of the dynamics taking place. Awareness truly is power. Once you are aware of something, you can never un-know it. It is at that point that it has become a part of you and your understanding. Once you gain this knowledge, you have the power to claim something greater for yourself, for your life, and for those in it, than you may have experienced before.

Your deepest desires no longer have to be delegated to the realm of wishful dreaming or hoping for better days. Once you understand the laws of nature, the nature of your mind and the nature of the deepest levels of your world, you can begin to rely upon something that is concrete and dependable and consistent.

You have the potential then to positively influence generations to come as your thoughts and ideas may be accepted as truth by those with whom you are influential. Your understanding of the workings of the world will begin to impact the collective consciousness until these laws are ultimately embedded in the consciousness of civilization.

When you allow yourself to productively use your imagination, essentially collapsing all alternative possibilities on a quantum level that do not support your imaginings, you are directly inputting your preferred new software into your mind. The importance of imagination cannot be underestimated as it is an enormously powerful tool of your inner most mind; your subconscious mind. As discussed, your subconscious mind is the place in your mind that holds all of the thoughts, feelings, and beliefs that you hold for yourself and what you determine is or isn't possible for yourself. It holds your emotions, habits, and memories as well as all of your unconscious bodily processes, working in the background as you go about your daily activities. It cannot tell the difference between something real or something imagined, and accepts everything it encounters as truth.

If we think of our mind as a computer and our thoughts and dreams as the software, the subconscious mind is then the computer's hard drive so to speak. Our subconscious mind does not concern itself with what type of software we run, what thoughts we think. It only accepts them at face value and will perform whatever program we have decided is appropriate at that moment. Additionally, no other thought programs may be performed while the current thought program is running. Once more, the choosing of a thought causes our possibilities to be collapsed down into only one possibility at any given point then.

In its simplicity, our subconscious mind doesn't care, or have the ability to determine, if we have never done something before, if we lack the skills, know what to do, or any other assortment of things we might imagine ourselves doing. It simply runs our imagination software as truth and then begins to act upon that truth.

The well-functioning computer of our mind will then search our environment and find all of those situations, people, events, and so on that match our chosen software. Good or bad, it will simply filter out everything that does not correlate with our thought software. It is our responsibility then, to choose the best programs to run in order to achieve our goals.

The freedom we are seeking is a state of mind. The outside world will always reflect what is taking place on the inside. It is one and the same. We must change the way we think about ourselves and our place in the world, because when positive thoughts and expectations are present, the mind begins to act accordingly. Once we change our inner dialogue, we ultimately change our reality.

In the words of Mahatma Gandhi, "Your beliefs become your thoughts; Your thoughts become your words; Your words become your actions; Your actions become your habits."

A great power resides within us which we only have to claim for it to be ours. When we allow ourselves to harness it we can unlock our potential and experience our possibilities!

Yet, the only way we can ever achieve the beautiful garden Claude Bristol refers to, is to first begin by choosing what we wish to harvest and then plant the appropriate seeds to reap that harvest. We can imagine each and every little thought and belief that we have as a tiny seed. Each little seed contains within itself the potential to become as big and beautiful or as harmful and prickly as it can possibly become. Then it must be planted in the fertile ground of our subconscious mind where it only needs to be nurtured a little for it to take root and start to grow. Then it must be watered and/or fed by continuing to focus our attention upon it. Finally, we must be patient, knowing that the seed we planted is growing as it should to produce itself.

As humans, we have been given the opportunity to determine the type of mental gardens we wish to cultivate. We can choose to be and experience all that we are capable of, or we can choose to be or have less. These fertile seeds possess the future, and whatever is planted will take root and grow.

We must find the seeds that are best suited to flower into our goals. A thistle will never grow to become a rose bush, so the importance of properly selecting our chosen seeds becomes imperative. As we begin to plant more and more positive and uplifting seeds (thoughts) in our fertile soil (our minds), then the possibilities of magnificence can come together and we will soon begin to reap what we have sown.

We can also allow ourselves to weed out those things that no longer serve us well. By doing so, we begin to tenderly nurture our goals, wishes, and dreams. When we encourage the beauty of our dreams to bloom and prosper, we can discover how quickly they will grow and multiply.

So, to plant a seed is to believe in the promise of tomorrow. Remembering that each type of seed will produce a specific type of outcome "tomorrow," enables us to choose with more clarity and certainty the type of harvest we choose to grow today. We then can become conscious co-creators in our lives.

Henry David Thoreau reminds us that repetition is a requirement for that promise to be fulfilled. "Just as a single footstep will not make a pathway on the earth, so a single thought will not make a pathway in the mind. To make a deep physical path, we walk again and again."

Your faithful thoughts will come to fruition. Ultimately, you must commit before Source will begin to bring your desires to you. The Universe will rearrange itself for your best and highest good the very instant you commit to the outcome. By law, there is no other alternative.

"Until one is committed, there is hesitancy," says William Hutchison Murray, "the chance to draw back, always ineffectiveness. Concerning all acts of initiative (and creation), there is one elementary truth, the ignorance of which kills countless ideas and splendid plans: that the moment one definitely commits oneself, then Providence moves too. All sorts of things occur to help one that would never otherwise have occurred. A whole stream of events issues from the decision, raising in one's favour all manner of unforeseen incidents and meetings and material assistance, which no man could have dreamt would have come his way. I have learned a deep respect for one of Goethe's couplets: Whatever you can do, or dream you can, begin it. Boldness has genius, power, and magic in it!"

Echoing the enlightened masters of our time, William James said, "Believe and your belief will actually create the fact." Your thoughts are acted upon according to the creative process of nature. Over and over throughout history we are told the nature of our world. Mind, body, spirit. Father, Son, Holy Ghost. Intelligence, Substance, Form. Alpha, omega, and everything in between. The trinity must be in harmony. Furthermore U.S. Anderson succinctly states that "When we finally realize that thought causes all, we will know that there are never any limits that we ourselves do not impose."

You do not attract what you want, but instead, you attract what you are. Your focus must be on only that which you desire, and never on the alternative. To do so will create a chaotic vibration that will produce a vibrational signal opposite to your desires. Furthermore, lack of clarity, inner struggle or conflict, and self-sabotage most definitely impede the successful realization of your preferred outcomes. The incongruence results in a mixed message that at its best can only produce a marginal result. The effectiveness of your thought vibration is greatly diminished.

The presence of fear or confusion undoubtedly produce a wobbly thought pattern, as it prevents the insight and awareness of the opportunities coming to you that would enable to direct manifestation of what you desire. You will get in your own way, then lament the fact that things don't work out for you or "aren't meant to be."

Everything that is in existence is in vibration and ruled by law. If it were not, our universe would be filled with chaos and disorder. Yet since law and vibration reign supreme, you can leverage an empowered mindset, the proper tools, and the scientific and spiritual principles operating in your life, so that it can become filled with miracles and magic.

A fixed or fearful mindset will surely prevent you from reaching you full potential. Often you can champion a growth mindset and positive thoughts for those around you, yet when it comes to yourself, combatting negativity often becomes much more difficult. You must become attentive and observant to the tone of your inner dialogue. Once you change your inner dialogue, you change your reality.

Yet there is a point that will inevitably arise out of consciously expanding to a greater version of yourself. It is the panic point, and it would be wise to prepare for its arrival. This is the moment when you have significantly moved out of your comfort zone and are shifting into a new dominant thought pattern.

In this breakdown-before-the-breakthrough, your mind will try everything it can to keep things the same. In the safety of what's known, as it fears for your survival. A cacophony of limiting and fear-based thoughts will flood your mind in the attempt to return to a state of familiar balance and certainty. The wave of thoughts will peak higher than ever before it ultimately extinguishes itself and becomes extinct.

Stay vigilant during this time, recognizing it for what it is; a last attempt of your former self to reclaim ownership of your thoughts. Recommit to your desired thoughts and outcomes, stay focused until the end. Indeed, stay focused. All of your power is in this moment. From the ashes of the panic point comes your greatest point of power. A greater version of yourself is being birthed. Have faith in the unseen and trust that your desires are on their way to you. Believe and surrender to the fact that you are being supported by the Universe. Be patient and look for signs, remembering that infinite intelligence will communicate with you often through your intuition.

You are limited only by your thoughts and imagination. The Universe will support you once you become clear and commit. Dare to dream beyond your wildest dreams and discover a richness of life that you never knew was possible.

CHAPTER 5 - YOUR DESIRES

What Do You Want?

We all want more. More for ourselves. More for our families. More for our lives. We want the ability to have more, be more, discover more, and do more. We want this life to be as full and enriching as we can possibly imagine it to be. Greater than that even.

You have been given one of the most amazing gifts in the world – the ability to choose what to think and feel and how to behave and ultimately to become the person you wish to become. The power of your mind makes this happen.

James Allen has told us you do not directly choose your circumstances, yet you have the power and ability to choose your thoughts, perceptions, beliefs, and behaviors and thereby shape and/or help to create your reality.

Perhaps the most difficult part is to consciously choose what it is you desire for yourself. Most of us, many times, float from one thing and then on to the next without really determining whether or not those things are serving our ultimate purpose or goals. We remain passive in life, waiting for the "good life" to suddenly drop into our laps without much effort on our part. We wait for the Fairy Godmother to wave her wand and magically make everything wonderful for us; to make all our dreams come true.

What we don't realize is that we are already holding our own magic wand and have been waving it around haphazardly this whole time. For better or for worse, your ignorance of how to properly command your wand through your words and your thoughts, and thereby your actions, has resulted in where you are today. The people you've surrounded yourself with, the situations you encounter, and the emotions you feel all stem from those magical words you utter to yourself and others.

You can awaken to the knowledge that you may be your own Fairy Godmother and begin to grant your own deepest desires. "You've always had it in you" as the Good Witch from The Wizard of Oz tells you. It doesn't matter where you are or how long you've been doing something or how old you are or what others may say or think. It simply begins with you choosing to take a more active role in the story of your life. It can begin today. In this moment. In fact, it will begin the moment you choose something new or something that is more in alignment with what you would like to experience. All things are possible to you at all times. All things are within your reach. There are no limits to what you are capable of doing, having, experiencing, or becoming.

That is at least until you choose. Then all other possibilities that don't support that choice become unavailable to you until you choose something different. Then once again all things become possible for you in that new moment.

You must only believe in yourself and your innate creative power, and you will discover that the magic is all around you.

The magic is within each and every one of us. There are no restrictions. None. The only restrictions you encounter are those you place upon yourself.

So in order for things to change, you must change. You must change the thoughts and ideas you hold for yourself. You must create an internal set point that is conducive to the life and reality you wish to experience. By doing so, you come to realize the wisdom in Emerson's assessment of the hardest task in the world. Only you might interpret his conclusion of thinking to include conscious thinking with a clear intention on that which is desired.

Of course, mental skills, methods, procedures, and techniques on how to continuously maintain conscious thought patterns of your desires continues to be ever evolving. However, with the underlying knowledge that you do indeed play a critical role in the life experiences you encounter and engage in, you now have an intimate understanding of how your thoughts can help create your best reality possible, and thus, it becomes your responsibility to choose wisely.

And so you have come full circle.

If you think the right thoughts, the world is at your feet. If you think the wrong thoughts, you doom yourself to pain, misery, and suffering.

It all sounds so easy. And it is.

Yet it is the most difficult thing in the world.

Nevertheless, it is the task you must master so that you may create the life you've dreamed for yourself, knowing that your thoughts truly do create your reality.

CHAPTER 6 - YOUR WORK

Implementing What You've Learned

So, what do you do with the knowledge you have just gained? It's one thing to know something; it's another to believe it in your heart and actually implement it into your life.

At your deepest levels of being, in the realm of your spirit, you are connected to everything there is. There is nothing you can do to sever this connection. Ever. Within your own being, you have a remarkable tool – the power of your mind – that allows you to tap into that deep and powerful place within. When you harness what has been divinely given, you unlock your potential and experience the possibilities.

Every day, throughout the day, allow yourself the opportunity to assess your level of connectedness to what it is you want for yourself. Give yourself permission to adopt and maintain a calmer and more peaceful state of mind, perhaps even despite your current surroundings.

Each night as you are falling asleep, and every morning

when you awaken, take a moment to connect with your innermost self. Affirm the outcomes you wish to achieve and allow your subconscious mind to activate the universal scientific and spiritual laws operating in the world.

Your intuitive self-direction and guidance will reveal itself much more clearly when you are in a relaxed state. Monitor the energetic frequency you are producing, making sure it corresponds to the physical manifestation you desire. Eliminate any negative thought patterns that arise the instant they are noticed. Act upon the impulses you receive from within if they are in alignment with your goals. Say yes to the opportunities that present themselves. Allow your life to be directed from a sense of knowingness that everything is happening as it should, in perfect order with Divine timing.

Creating a mindset capable of producing miracles and magic requires a growth in your consciousness. You must be willing to expand yourself beyond what you have been up to this point. It requires honesty. It requires openness and a level of personal ownership that may at first feel uncomfortable. It requires faith. Most of all, it requires a deep level of trust that you have more power than the power you have claimed, and that your Source will grant you your deepest desires if only you have the courage to ask.

I invite you to ask.

Ask for those things you hold most dear and close to your heart. Ask for those things that you long for in the quiet moments of the night. Ask for those things that are secret to everyone but you and your soul. Ask for them. All of them. Miracles and magic will unfold once you do.

CHAPTER 7 - YOUR PRACTICE

*S*pecific *Discussions on Focus Areas with Meditations*

Throughout the following pages, you'll discover numerous visualization and guided meditations meant to enhance the understanding of the messages provided in this book. Use them to facilitate a shift in your thought patterns to a mindset of growth, oneness, and openness.

Remember, your responsibility in the creation of your desires is to get clear on what it is that you would like to do, have, be, or experience. "Don't worry about the how. It is all taken care of for you as long as you do your part of thinking, acting, speaking, and being in accordance with that dream. Just dream, visualize, and then start doing something." David Cameron Gikandi reminds us that not only are we to dream and visualize, but we also must take action.

Still, while you are positively expecting your great results, surrender with a feeling of gratitude and certainty that the thing you desire is already yours, is on its way, and will arrive at the most perfect moment.

It is the responsibility of Source to bring your desires to you in whatever shape or form is for your best and highest good. When it does present itself, you must say yes to receive it.

As you begin to establish a routine of time dedicated to your inner work, you may find the following information useful as a guideline.

Locate a quiet place where you will be uninterrupted. It should be a time where you can focus only upon yourself for a while, without worry about timelines and schedules. Turn off any potential sources of distraction such as your telephone or computer.

Perhaps begin by putting on some calming music; the kind that you can listen to and immediately feel a shift of slowing down taking place within your mind and body. Music that effortlessly stirs your soul. Allow those soft tones to move you into a more peaceful place as you perhaps light a candle and invite a greater level of awareness and wisdom to come to you.

Remind yourself that this is a time when nobody wants anything from you and nobody expects anything from you. You can simply offer this gift of time, inner focus, and reflection as an opportunity to learn and explore the power within you. It is a chance to reconnect to the deeper you who has always been there, just perhaps buried or forgotten. Now is the time to exhume and polish your innate grandeur. When you do, you will sit in awe at the beauty of it and all that awaits you.

As you begin to relax, find a comfortable position to sit or lie in and maybe place a blanket over yourself to keep warm. You may wish to have someone read these meditations to you or you could record yourself and play it back. You may also choose to imagine a wise guide, spiritual figure, someone you trust, or even your deepest self, is whispering these words to you and speaking directly to the level of your spirit.

Let that voice be heard within so that your core resonates with the truth of who you are and what you are capable of accomplishing.

This is a process of learning to connect with your deepest and innermost self. Be gentle with yourself. If you have random thoughts enter into your mind as you are relaxing, simply let them be. Don't try to fight them. Fighting them will only give them your energy and make them stronger and more plentiful. Observe that they are there and then return your awareness back to the meditation. Without energy, they will disperse. Remember you are in control and choose what to focus on and where to put your energy. The more you practice, the easier it will become.

I wish you all the best.

And so you begin...

MEDITATIONS

INNER FOCUS

"*If You Believe It, You Can Achieve It*"

No powerful experience can occur in the mind without some measurable influence on the body. Therefore, it must be possible to explain the mechanism of inner focus, trance, and suggestion in terms of real events that happen in the body.

On average, any given nerve cell in the human brain interconnects with 5,000 other nerve cells. The number of possible interconnections between the nerve cells in the human body is huge, but finite. Your body's way to simplify this process is to "kindle" the nerve cells. Nerves that are frequently used via your thoughts, feelings, and behaviors, have a slightly positive charge. With repetition, the nerve path becomes kindled, or programmed, and your body begins to respond automatically. Habits are formed when the subconscious part of the mind takes control of your thoughts, feelings, and behaviors, and you no longer have to consciously think about how to react to something.

In a deeply relaxed state such as meditation, hypnosis, and guided visualizations, a change occurs in the structure of your brain that links the two halves of the brain. This change causes more information to flow from one side of your brain to the other than would normally be the case.

During this time, nerve cells in the part of your brain that control habits lose some of their electrical charge, and your mind becomes more subject to change. Using imagery and suggestion, new connections among the nerve cells can be kindled or bundled together.

There are four different states of brainwave activity; all are measured in Hertz (HZ), a unit of frequency equal to once cycle per second. Beta is experienced in normal waking time when you are active and alert (14-30 HZ). Alpha is experienced when you are relaxed (8-12 HZ). The majority of all visualization and hypnosis takes place in this state of activity. Theta is experienced when you are daydreaming, have good imagery and reverie, or are at near sleep (3-7 HZ). This is the frequency where you dream while you sleep. Medical and dental procedures including some surgeries can also take place without the use of anesthetic at this depth of inner focus. Lastly, Delta is the slowest frequency (1-3 HZ), when you are in deep and dreamless sleep.

If you are concerned about your ability to be successful, it is helpful if you avoid analyzing the process or trying to determine how deeply focused you are because you simply won't be able to tell. You can be assured, however, that the results you will receive afterward will indicate your level of success. But it most definitely is a skill that you will strengthen with time and experience.

By learning and incorporating meditation, visualization, self-hypnosis, and inner focus into your life, you are giving yourself a wonderful gift. All aspects of your life including your personal growth, existing challenges, and desired goals can be addressed with these tools, and very soon you will discover the guidance of your own inner wisdom and the whisperings of the Universe.

You must be in a state of calm, peace, and trust to consciously connect with your subconscious. A sense of fear or apprehension will effectively block any successful attempt you may have at changing an existing thought pattern.

Remind yourself that you are in control of the process. If you enjoy the sensations of calm and relaxation that you experience during your inner focus, let yourself open to an even greater sense of those feelings. If you enjoy the insight and awareness that you receive during your times of inner focus, allow yourself to expand to an even deeper level of those offerings as well.

The focus of your work with your subconscious mind is so that whatever you would like to change or improve, you will be able to achieve those results and with a greater sense of ease and assurance of your desired outcomes.

Remember, when positive expectations and emotions are present, the mind begins to act accordingly and thereby activates the underlying scientific and spiritual principles of the world to bring about the external manifestation of your desires.

VISUALIZATION - STEPS TO INNER FOCUS

*B*egin by placing your thumb and index finger together. This acts as a trigger to your mind and body that you are beginning your inner focus. As you move thorough your meditation, your fingers may naturally separate as your mind and body relax. Simply allow this to happen. It is only necessary to place them together when you initiate your inner focus.

Take a deep breath and hold it. Roll your eyes up as if you were trying to look at the top of your head. Your eyes may begin to flutter. Now keeping your eyes up, slowly close your eyelids. Exhale and relax your eyes, relax your body. You will feel a wave of relaxation flow over you. It is possible to fight it, but that defeats the purpose.

Now focus your attention inward. Allow your eyes to remain closed, and imagine you are in front of a staircase or in an elevator, whichever you prefer. Notice that there are 25 steps (or floors). With each slow step you take, you will move more deeply and easily within yourself. As you move upon the stairs, silently repeat phrases to yourself such as, "going down into deeper relaxation, going down, down, letting go," and so on. At the base of the stairs is a large, cushy, allergy-free, feather bed. On the last stair, you will simply sink into that bed, resting your head the comfortable pillow. If you are using the elevator, the doors can open to your favorite place in nature.

As you are deeply relaxing in the cushy bed, or if you are somewhere in nature, initially start out by giving yourself the following suggestion: "Every day, in every way, I'm getting better and better." Repeat this affirmation at least ten times.

If you would rather create your own specific affirmations, keep in mind the six key elements all affirmations must contain in order to be effective. They must be positive, present tense, measurable, simple, believable, and carry a reward. Make sure to develop your own affirmations while in the awake state to ensure all six elements are included.

Alternatively, you can choose to use the time you are relaxing in the cushy bed or in your place in nature, as a time for inner guidance, self-discovery, or to connect with All That Is.

After giving yourself the affirmations, or your inner focus work, you may slowly count yourself up from 1 to 5 to the awake state, or you may choose to fall asleep if you are practicing your meditation at night.

Enjoy the process. Be gentle with yourself, and know that all shall be well.

ABUNDANCE

"*My Life Overflows with Abundance*"

Your innate desire for expansion and growth creates a never-ending desire for greater abundance in all shapes and sizes.

Often you can find yourself looking at the world, tapped into this desire for more, and witness lack and longing for what's not visible and present. If you are not careful, you can begin to focus upon the things that have not yet aligned with your desires and manifested into reality.

Yet you can be sure the moment you develop that desire, you have begun to activate the Universal laws which foretell its arrival. The Universe is ever-expanding and always in a state of abundance and plenty. You must only train yourself to observe the abundance in and all around you in every moment.

We come from a place where anything and everything is possible. Where there are no boundaries or limitations;

where everything is wholesome, pure and true. This is the source of everything; of all the things in our world.

Yet you can often get in your own way and block the connection to the presence of abundance that is available to you in every moment. It requires a shift into a more empowering mindset and ridding yourself of those things that limit you. You will live into your fullest potential, or not, depending upon your thoughts and what you focus on. You can change a thought, so you can change a belief that is not supporting you.

When you have the desire to do more, have more, and be more in abundance, you must begin by challenging all negative beliefs that begin to surface around it. Observe the abundance that exists in your world; there is so much available for you to reflect upon.

Recall the endless blades of grass, the leaves on the trees, the fur or feathers upon an animal, the grains of sand in the desert and upon the shore, the brilliant stars in the sky, the cells that create your body, the drops of rain in a storm, the fish in the sea, the animals in the forest, the sparkles of light that dance upon the water, the breaths you take in a single day, the beats of your heart, the words in a book, the possibilities are themselves plentiful and endless.

A shift into the recognition of abundance within and around you can remind you that you, and the world, are more than you, and it, appears to be.

This visualization exercise will allow you to tap into the connection to abundance that awaits you in every moment.

VISUALIZATION - 10,000 FORESTS

*T*ake a deep breath, and as you exhale, allow yourself to get a little more comfortable and a little more relaxed. Let go of any tension or tightness in your neck or shoulders, and notice the way your eyes feel right now. Allow your eyelids to get heavy, loose, and relaxed. Perhaps you'd like to close your eyes right now or maybe you would like to in a few moments when it feels just right for you... knowing there is nothing you need to do, nowhere for you to be, nobody is wanting anything from you, nobody is expecting anything from you.

So you can just allow yourself to perhaps become aware of the sounds around you, and you can allow those sounds to begin to relax you. Allow those sounds to float in and out of your awareness, and allow the muscles of your body to relax so deeply and completely, as you become more relaxed than you could possibly imagine.

Let your body breathe so very softly, gently. Notice that each breath effortlessly floats in and then out of your body, and every time you exhale you relax into those sounds around you, breathing so easily, softly, slowly. Anytime you'd like to

relax deeper, you take a breath, and as you exhale you go even deeper within into that perfect and peaceful place of home.

As you allow your body and mind to relax in this perfect and peaceful place, you know this is a place where you can go for wisdom, learning, and truth. In this still and silent place within, you can tap into your deeper self. You can dip into the bliss of possibilities where anything is within your reach. The possibilities are each like an acorn, where each action and every decision can grow strong and mighty and larger than life if nourished and cared for.

Allow your infinitely wise mind to select an acorn of abundance that will demonstrate just one of the possibilities available to you. Plant it in the fertile soil of your mind and let it take you to a time and place where you are clearly living, breathing, and being abundant.

Let your mind fill with thoughts of your abundance. Let them float on words of ease and grace and gratitude.

Let your heart overflow with an abundance of love and compassion, kindness and caring, so that you are filled from within, and allow it to flow outwardly into the world.

Let your hands touch into your world of abundance, offering you a tangible proof of all that you have successfully created.

Let your eyes see the magnificence that is here, as you see through the eyes of your abundance and plenty.

Let yourself taste the flavor of your life and smell the fragrance of pride and accomplishment at all that is before you.

Let your ears hear the sound of your own voice saying the words that validate your abundance, and the sounds around you echoing their agreement.

Breathe it all in deeply and know that you have planted your acorn deeply. Your foundation will nourish and support your growth, and at the most perfect moment you will discover the 10,000 forests of abundance you have created because you became all that you were meant to become; and it all started when you planted your single acorn of possibilities.

Take a nice big deep breath. Let it out and let yourself come back to your surroundings. Trusting that this acorn has been planted, and you can allow it to manifest into a new form of the abundance that is within and around you now. And so it is.

BEAUTY

"*I See Myself Surrounded by Beauty*"

There is astounding grace and beauty in the world. Everything has its place. Everything has its purpose. Everything is created with the most perfect attributes to enable a complete expression of its essence.

The perfection with which the world has been created and all those things within it demonstrates an underlying consciousness that is omniscient and infallible. It is something that can be seen with the eyes, felt with the heart, and lived with the soul. It is a multidimensional phenomenon who's magnitude may never be fully comprehended by the human mind.

Yet, you are an integral part of that beautiful perfection.

You are meant to shine your light in the world as beautifully and brightly as the Divine spark within you. Your experiences are offered to you as a platform from which you may dive deeper into your true self and experience yourself more fully.

Yet sometimes you have allowed your experiences in life to leave a shadow upon your light. You may have forgotten the beauty of simple things; forgotten the beauty that is within you. Your eyes may be blind to witnessing that beauty if you are focused on what may seemingly appear to be out of place or different from your expectations. Any flaws or perceived failures are a figment of the mind; a perception that has lost its connection with the Divine within. Just like the pearl that develops from an irritation within the oyster, sometimes the most beautiful things originate from a small speck out of place, and yet truly in the most perfect place.

A shift back into your authentic self will allow you to tap into the peaceful perfection of the beauty within and all around you in every single moment, trusting that the here and now will deliver you to something truly magnificent. As is everything else, it is a choice of what you choose to see and believe.

This visualization exercise will allow you to reconnect to the beauty, within yourself and within the world, that is perpetually available to you at all times.

VISUALIZATION - MERMAID CASTLE

*T*ake a deep breath, and as you exhale, allow yourself to get a little more comfortable and a little more relaxed. Let go of any tension or tightness in your neck or shoulders, and notice the way your eyes feel right now. Allow your eyelids to get heavy, loose, and relaxed. Perhaps you'd like to close your eyes right now or maybe you would like to in a few moments when it feels just right for you... knowing there is nothing you need to do, nowhere for you to be, nobody is wanting anything from you, nobody is expecting anything from you.

So you can just allow yourself to perhaps become aware of the sounds around you, and you can allow those sounds to begin to relax you. Allow those sounds to float in and out of your awareness, and allow the muscles of your body to relax so deeply and completely, as you become more relaxed than you could possibly imagine.

Let your body breathe so very softly, gently. Notice that each breath effortlessly floats in and then out of your body, and every time you exhale you relax into those sounds around you, breathing so easily, softly, slowly. Anytime you'd like to

relax deeper, you take a breath, and as you exhale you go even deeper within into that perfect and peaceful place of home.

As you allow your body and mind to relax in this perfect and peaceful place, you know this is a place where you can go for wisdom, learning, and truth. Out before you, in your mind's eye, the scene slowly begins to come into focus. You discover yourself, standing upon the edge of the shore with only thoughts of peace and comfort.

As your gaze stretches out, you notice the shimmer of the water as the sun shines upon it and makes it sparkle like diamonds. There is a gentle breeze that feels like a thousand kisses upon your skin. The waves lapping against your toes in the water sounds as if it is singing you a soft melody that lulls you into a deeper state of peace and contentment. You intuitively sense it is a magical day in every possible way.

As you breathe in the salty air and relax into the sounds around you, a movement in the water draws your attention. You patiently watch for signs... and as if in a fairy tale, before you in the water emerges a mermaid. Without a word she invites you closer. There is an unspoken trust between you that is beyond words. You sense it deep within yourself that the beautiful being before you is your teacher... your guide to a new level of understanding and wisdom.

Into her extended hand you place yours, and the world becomes illuminated from within. It is as though you are witnessing the true essence... the spirit... of everything around you. Somehow it is as if you are seeing with fresh eyes the beauty that is before you... around you... and within you.

She knowingly squeezes your hand as you nod your head in gratitude and look into her eyes, you affirm you are ready. You sense a subtle shift in your energy as her magic envelops you.

With a gentle movement, you are immediately transported to her underwater world. Your surroundings hold a beauty that can be felt with your heart as you connect to the world around you.

The colors here are so vibrant and pure. The sounds are musical and magical with a melody your heart somehow already knows. The rhythm flows through your body like an old friend that leaves you feeling light and free. You can almost taste the beauty of the world.

As you breathe it in, you can sense the beauty within you. Tune into this beauty and notice how you allow it to flow from you. As it does, it impacts all that it encounters, and it fills you with joy. You understand the more you allow the beauty within to shine, the more brightly the world itself shines and becomes.

With this awareness, the mermaid comes close and touches over your heart... reminding you that beauty comes from within, and is reflected in the world back to you in return.

You take it in as you take another deep breath in, promising to shine your light more brightly for all to see.

Your next breath finds you back on land in your world with the whisper of your promise still echoing across your lips and heart. And it fills you with such joy...

Now slowly bring your awareness back to your surroundings, and open your eyes to the beauty within and all around you.

BELIEVE

"*I Believe in the Beauty of My Dreams*"

You are here on purpose with a purpose, for a purpose. Your dreams and desires are not random. They are a calling from the Diving through your deepest Self. They are the method through which you may manifest the unfolding of your purposed, enabling the successful expansion of consciousness within and without.

With the desires comes the means for its complete fulfillment. All things are possible. All things are within your reach. You must only believe in yourself, and you will find that the magic is all around you. The magic is within you.

However, your life experiences have often not reflected this Divine magic. Often you have encountered fear and lack which have limited the realization of your potential. Yet all of life is simply a series of lessons which have brought you to this point in time and space. The delays, roadblocks, and misdirections will all benefit the perfection of Divine timing.

Your development and acceptance of your skills, abilities, and talents are the blueprint to living your life on purpose.

Your light shining as a beacon can chase away the shadows of another as you step into your fullness. The light you cast can spark greatness in all whom you encounter. Yet the light that will uplift the world begins when you believe in your truth. When you believe in your innate value, worth, and importance, your life will open to greater ease as you align with the Divine flow of the Universe.

Henry David Thoreau teaches us that "As a single footstep will not make a pathway on the earth, so a single thought will not make a pathway in the mind. To make a deep physical path, we walk again and again."

This visualization exercise will allow you to nurture yourself with the qualities that will allow your light to shine even more brightly when they are embraced more fully. Absorb it and allow yourself to fill with a greater knowingness of who you truly are. Then walk this path again and again.

VISUALIZATION - CONFIDENCE CAKE

*S*it comfortably. Take a deep breath and as you allow yourself to settle more deeply into a relaxed position, you can allow your body and mind to begin to become a little more peaceful and a little more relaxed. This time, here in this moment, is just for you. A time to connect to that calm and peaceful place that is always within you. So just allow your breath to become so very soft and gentle, flowing so very easily and effortlessly.

As your body and mind continue to become more relaxed and at ease with each passing breath, you can allow your mind to float and drift to a familiar kitchen. You notice all the details in this place that just make you feel right at home, and at ease, knowing you can truly let your guard down and be yourself completely here... in this moment. The colors, the sounds, the smells of this kitchen are indeed very welcome to you.

Notice the presence of another beside you. There beside you is the most loving and giving person you know. Mountains would be moved for you, such is their love and devotion to you. You trust this person completely and know that you are always in a safe place whenever you are with them, where time and space do not matter. You trust this person always has your best interest at heart and will guide you to where you need to be, whenever you need it. You trust that you will never be lead astray by what is offered to you.

As you notice all the details of this loving person, in this relaxing kitchen, notice their eyes. A special gleam shines forth with a bit of mystery, and you know there is a grand plan at work here, behind the scenes. Something that will come to you and be revealed when the moment is right. Until then, you bask in the loving connection between the two of you.

You hear this person proclaim there is to be a celebration, and for it to be a proper celebration, you must make a cake. You eagerly agree and discover you are to make a cake of confidence. You've never heard of it before, but know that you will be guided by the loving wisdom with you. And so you gather your supplies, prepare your surface, make ready for the making of magic.

You hear the sound of their voice guiding you, step by step, and yet the sound of their voice echoes as the sound of your own voice, which somehow echoes throughout your body and resonates into the core of your being. You hear the sound of the loving voices and they say...

Add one large heaping of self-confidence. Curious, you look to your loved one who nods their encouragement and approval, and so you add one large heaping and continue with greater confidence.

Add a large measure of belief in yourself. You again look inquiringly to your loved one who nods their encouragement and approval, and so you continue adding more belief in yourself.

Begin to knead trust, value, and worth together into the

batter of your uniqueness, and shape it into an inner strength that is nourishing.

Last comes self-love. Dissolve any impurities... peel away self-doubt and insecurities. Reduce them down to their true essence. Pour in all the love that can fit within, and as you do, the love flows into all the empty spaces... filling it completely. Your loved one gives you a squeeze of acknowledgement and affection. You feel the love overflowing within and without.

Allow the ingredients to marinate completely, infusing their characters into the others so that all can be experienced at the same time... so that none are out of balance... All are in perfect proportions to support your healthy growth and development on all levels of your being... mentally, physically, spiritually. Blend them to encourage expansion in the most perfect way.

With a wave of their hand, the confidence cake is ready... a sacred and special gift for you. Your loved one guides you to a special place where you take a bite of the confidence cake you created and allow it to nourish and sustain you as you move forward from this moment... filled with confidence, inner strength, courage, trust, value and worth... a newfound belief in yourself, your uniqueness, in your voice... and it fills you with trust and motivation, and a deep desire to take action on the thing that is calling within.

Share your voice and your gift with all those you encounter, and know you are feeding them with love and light. As you do, you experience the sweet fragrance of pride and purpose fill you within and motivate you to fulfill your passion.

And so it is.

CHANGE

"*Magical Moments Are Eagerly Waiting*"

The Universe is constantly changing and expanding, shifting and finding new balance. It is such a significantly vital force of life that should it stop, life comes to an end. Change is a natural and necessary part of growth, development, and transition.

Every experience you've had in your life has shaped and impacted you in some way. Perhaps some have been more pleasing and desirable than others, yet each has molded you into this very moment, into the 'you' of today. You have a choice whether to fight it or flow with the ever-present change.

You can choose to avoid change by turning your back upon the truth. You can allow your insecurities to cause you to pretend everything is as it was, even as your world shifts around you. Meanwhile, you will be forced to stuff your thoughts and emotions inward, never rocking the boat for fear you will be unable to handle it if others knew of your vulnerability. But you can only stuff yourself so much before you explode and lash out either destructively toward yourself or defensively against others, all the while hoping that if you fight hard enough the change will disappear. When you fight the change, you hold a negative expectation that a loss of some magnitude will occur if the change is allowed to occur.

Alternatively, you can choose to throw open your arms and welcome the uncertainty and chaos wholeheartedly, trusting yourself and the situation to unfold with ease and grace. You can choose to believe you will grow in ways you would not have been able to without it. Opportunities are discovered as doors are opened and new life chapters are written. The positive expectation you hold when you are in an internal place of trust, is that all shall be well and for your best and highest good.

Still you may often find yourself somewhere in between. Wherever you are on the spectrum, that is the right place for you at this moment in time. Creating an awareness of your mindset will allow you to shift into the expectation that each change is an opportunity to learn and grow. Learn to embrace the unknown and you will discover magical moments unfolding before you that will lead to somewhere that wouldn't have been possible without it.

This visualization exercise will allow you to gain a bit of hindsight into your current life. Perhaps there are things you would benefit from changing in your life, even if it is just a new perspective. The answers always come when you take the time to listen. Most importantly, always act upon the information and make the necessary changes.

VISUALIZATION - DARKNESS TO LIGHT

*T*ake a nice big deep breath, and as you exhale, allow yourself to settle into a comfortable position. As you take another deep breath and allow yourself to begin to relax, in your mind's eye and in your imagination, step into a dark room. This is a room you have spent much time in. You are calmed and comforted by its familiarity and all the hidden details contained within... you know it intimately... and it almost seems as though the darkness was a part of you. You have grown used to the darkness. In the darkness it is difficult to see and feel where you are going... often bumping into things... bouncing around... sometimes even causing you to stumble and fall.

In order to protect yourself from getting hurt, you may have stopped moving forward... or perhaps even started going in circles. And through it all, you have always known that there has to be a way out... trusting and always believing that there is a way to return to the light... and once again see yourself as you truly are.

You now know that you have to move through the darkness in order to find your light... and your true self... at the other end. The journey is not far... it is a quick journey. Nor are you fearful or apprehensive because you feel so safe and secure at all times... comforted by the knowledge that this quick healing journey is indeed necessary if you still wish to make positive changes in your life. To become the person you were meant to be. Completely whole and complete. And you wonder why anyone would choose to remain stagnant... lost in the dark... never moving forward. This awareness brings you confidence and peace of mind as you reaffirm your desire to move forward and leave the darkness behind you.

And so you are beginning to see and feel within the very depths of your mind, body, and spirit exactly how this darkness has captivated and contained you. Perhaps you are aware of what caused the darkness to settle upon you. Perhaps this awareness remains unconscious. But whichever way it is for you, know that it continues to reveal itself to you in whatever way is most appropriate. The more you experience all levels of this darkness, the more you understand its purpose... consciously and unconsciously. Perhaps it represents a fear of failure, fear of success, a lack of self-confidence, or even a sense of unworthiness or value. Whatever the darkness represents, with your newfound understanding comes a sense that the darkness is lifting... and so you begin to move forward.

With each step forward you feel a new sense of self-confidence and determination... to move beyond your old limitations and to embrace the possibilities of what may lie in your future. Feel yourself experiencing a surge of curiosity and excitement at what you may find ahead, as you continue on your journey.

Suddenly you find yourself on the other side of your room, and have reached a light switch. And you realize that it is not necessary to know exactly how you moved through the darkness and overcame the obstacles that once held you back, but you now only feel a sense of pride and accomplishment that you finally did it. This light switch, once turned on, will allow you to see your surroundings very clearly. You will see the obstacles that once held you back. You will embrace those qualities and characteristics that will enable you to achieve the kind of life you are seeking. You will hear the sounds of success cheering you on to greatness. You will feel the emotion and personal satisfaction of this beautiful moment.

On the count of three, you will turn on your light and embrace the beauty of what was always there, but had been hidden. Prepare yourself for an amazing discovery. 1... 2... 3 (snap). As the light comes on and shines brightly all around you, the light reaches all corners and depths of this place. There is no darkness... only light remains. Your light grows stronger and shines brighter as your acceptance of your light is affirmed. The more you dwell upon the light that is within you, the more it grows within you. As you continue to bask in the warmth of the light that is you, your awareness becomes focused on the details of the previously darkened room. The details reveal themselves as you now clearly see what was once hidden. You are standing in a room filled with everything you could possibly imagine.

Notice before you is a mirror. Step in front of that mirror and observe your reflection. Identify anything that remains on or attached to you that you'd like to remove... anything that may slow you down or get you stuck. This is your time to clean off old aspects of yourself that are no longer benefiting you. Find a way to shed any remaining negativity or darkness that has weighted you down, held you back, caused you to move in circles or remain stagnant. Feel the release of negativity and burden as they are shed. You feel lighter, more energetic, and full of life and excitement.

Now once again observe your reflection in the mirror, and notice that your mind, body, and spirit is clean and pure.

With a new sense of freedom and unending possibilities before you, search your room for those things you'd like to take with you and make a part of you. As you search this place you find many things you thought you could never possess – but everything you could ever want is all here. Those skills, tools... thoughts, feelings and beliefs... the knowledge and wisdom you'd like to incorporate into your being... find them and make them a part of you. Some of them like self-confidence, pride, wisdom, and a belief of worthiness quickly merge with your mind, body, and spirit. Others you can carry along with you or wear without a feeling of burden.

When you have gathered and incorporated all the beneficial characteristics and qualities into your being, return to the mirror. Notice those negative things you shed laying pitifully upon the floor, and how you no longer have any room or desire to carry them with you. You now are positively whole and plentiful. Wise and self-assured. Beautiful inside and out. Feel how magnificent it is to be in balance and harmony with yourself again. You do deserve this.

Ready to move forward, to embrace the new possibilities that await you ahead, you notice a door that leads to your future. You realize in all aspects of your mind, body, and spirit that the future is of your creation. You've released the parts of your past that no longer served you, so that you could welcome and incorporate the positive things into your life. The future is yours... you have all the skills, tools... thoughts, feelings and beliefs... the knowledge and wisdom necessary to move forward to an even more amazing life. Step through the door to your future and embrace what lies ahead.

FLOW

"*Do Not Fight the Flow, for it Leads Me to Something Wonderful*"

There is a rhythm of the Universe. A metaphorical guiding hand that brings experiences and others into your life with perfect Divine timing. Often these spiritual encounters fulfill sacred contracts that enable you to grow exponentially. There are profound opportunities for personal expansion or redirection with every individual, obstacle, roadblock, or smooth path brought before you. Still, you have a choice in how you perceive the experiences of your life. You can fight or you can flow.

At times life can seem raw, gritty and seemingly dark. It can feel as if you have lost control, lost your way, lost your purpose, lost your Self. As the chaos spirals around you, you wonder which way is up; which way will lead you out of the confusion and back into happiness and fulfillment; back to peace and calm.

If only you could bury your head in the sand and know

that things will be better when you return. If only you could pull the covers over your head until the ugly monsters have moved on. If only you could find the magic bullet, the quick fix, the genie in the bottle to snap everything back into place. If only. If only.

If only you allowed yourself to explore the circumstances around you with open eyes. If only you gave yourself permission to feel what it is you feel deep inside. If only you found the courage to move through the darkness and rediscover yourself. If only you believe the Universe is working with you and for you. It is then that you will find that your life becomes joyous, uplifting and bright.

A Course in Miracles says "Nothing real can be threatened. Nothing unreal exists. Herein lies the peace of God." The monsters you fear, you have unintentionally created. They are an illusion. Yet you have the ability to shift into trust and love, move beyond the facades that have appeared in your life, and return to the flow.

This visualization exercise will allow you to let go of your expectations of how things should be, so you can embrace the unfolding of every moment with greater ease and grace.

VISUALIZATION - LET GO

*T*ake a deep breath. Let the world around you soften and begin to lose its edges. Let every breath you breathe fill you with a sense of peace and comfort. Let your every exhale release any tension or tightness. Take this moment, right here, right now, to be guided by the inner wisdom that is within you always. Inhale. Exhale. Just breathe.

Imagine you are somewhere in nature on a beautiful day. Notice the sounds around you. Notice what time of day it is. Notice the temperature is perfect and exactly as you wish it to be.

Notice all the thoughts that are swirling in your mind, asking for your attention. For now, you can give yourself permission to set them aside. If any are important to you they can be there for you if you choose to claim them again. Now is a time for you to just be here, now. In this very moment.

So allow your thoughts to be soft and gentle, still and free, as you bring your attention to the surroundings of nature, here in this perfect and peaceful place.

Notice somewhere nearby is the sound of a stream. The

sound draws you near and you feel a deeper sense of relaxation flow within you as it comes into view. It is a meandering stream that flows with ease and grace. Its rhythm is mesmerizing and you feel yourself loosen and release areas within that were tangled and blocked.

Breathe in deeply and let go.

You follow the stream to the place where the gentle water flows over a waterfall. It makes a palpable sound that blocks all other sound from your awareness. Its powerful roar lulls you into a cadence of relaxation and inner focus. You feel yourself calm and settle and slow. The rush stills you inside as the water churns and flows, bringing to the surface those things that are ready to release and be carried away.

The spray nourishes the rocks and growth beside it as the white water streams down three more gentle falls. The foam and speed slowing downriver as it passes the life it helps to sustain. You sense the birds and forest animals that are here with you as you watch the stream flow around a bend and out of sight.

From somewhere nearby, an animal reveals itself to you. It may be immediately clear where this animal is or perhaps it may need some gentle encouragement. But it has come here for you, to offer a message to help you understand something new.

The deep wisdom of this animal guide resonates with truth.

Ask this animal, "What message do you have to share with me today?" Then wait and listen for the answer, knowing it will communicate with you in the most appropriate way for you to completely understand. After it answers you, say thank you.

Being with this animal provides a deep level of peace, openness, and trust.

Ask the animal, "What is the most important thing I

need to do or release in this moment in time?" Then wait for the answer. Be sure to thank it once it has finished, and then allow it to leave, surrounded in an air of gratitude and love.

Allow yourself to integrate this new understanding and trust into all levels of your mind, body, and spirit. Breathe in deeply and open your eyes when you are ready.

I AM

"I Am All that I Ever Was"

St. Francis understood that "What we are looking for is who is looking." You are the great Divine wrapped in a human body, yet have disconnected from this deepest and most authentic truth.

There is a beautiful myth that illustrates our depth and resistance to all that we truly are. It is called "Where Shall We Hide the Spirit of God?"

"Where shall we hide the Spirit of God from people?" the gods all cried when they were made. "How can we guard our secret now?" they asked each other so afraid.

"Hide our Spirit in the earth and they will mine it. Hide it on a mountain and they will climb it. Even in the sea they will find it. Where, oh where, shall we hide the Spirit of God from people?"

"Hide our Spirit in the wind and they will pursue it. Hide it in an atom and they will view it. Even in an act they will do it. Where, oh where, shall we hide the Spirit of God from people?"

They thought of stars in outer space or in the nature of a tree, but they knew that people could solve each and every mystery.

"Hide our Spirit in matter and they will analyze it. Hide it in water and they will crystallize it. Even in hell they will surmise it. Where, oh where, shall we hide the Spirit of God from people?"

And then they solved the puzzle of how the frightened gods should win. After a long discussion, the wisest said, "Let us take the Spirit of God and hide it deep inside of them, for this will be the last place they will look to find it."

"Hide our Spirit in their heart and they will doubt it. Hide our Spirit in their very soul and they will live without it. Even if we reveal it and shout it, they will never, never believe that the Spirit of God is deep inside of them."

"This discovery will not be made until they have all the experience necessary to complete a well-rounded life."

The revered philosophical masters of the ages have repeatedly spoken the truth in their teachings that we are all Divine and intimately responsible for and connected to the grandeur around us.

Erich Fromm teaches that "Man's main task in life is to give birth to himself." It is time for you believe in all that you are. It is time that you claim your power and abilities. It is time that you remember the truth of your innermost self and divinity, so that you may more deeply fulfill the purpose you are here for. The time is now for you to seek and embrace your power within... for it is only there that you may truly know yourself and become whole.

Meister Eckhart has God speaking to us saying, "I became God for you. If you do not become God for me, you do me wrong."

Sometimes we get confused about who we really are. As we go through life, we often acquire thoughts, beliefs, and perceptions from those around us. We mistake the things we have, the way we look, our friends and family, our job, and our current problems and situations with our value. We forget that these things are not who we really are. Who is it that you are deep within? Beyond all the masks and confusions, who are you when you are alone?

This visualization exercise will allow you to remind yourself that you are more than those things, and that you have a choice in how you will live your life.

VISUALIZATION - THE PURPLE BAG

*G*et into a comfortable position and allow your eyes to gently close. Take a deep breath, and when you're ready, exhale slowly and allow your body to relax...

Take another deep breath. Exhale slowly and allow yourself to feel calm, peaceful and relaxed. This time is just for you. At this moment, there is no place you need to go; nothing else you need to do; nothing else you need to think about. Allow your mind to become far away from bothersome concerns. Your calmness increases and your mind becomes more and more at peace and at ease. The comfort spreads throughout every part of your body, and any discomfort becomes less and less and less. Inhale deeply and hold it for three or four seconds, and then exhale slowly. As you inhale, you bring more oxygen into your body, and as you exhale it causes your body to keep relaxing more and more. Continue breathing easily and effortlessly, and feel yourself becoming more calm and peaceful.

Now place your awareness on your eyelids. You know that you can relax those eyes beautifully. You know that you can relax your eyelids so deeply that as long as you choose to not remove that relaxation, your eyelids just won't work. And when you know you've relaxed your eyes so deeply and completely, hold on to that relaxation. If you like, you can test them and notice how wonderful it feels that you are in control or you can just allow yourself to continue to enjoy the beautiful feelings of relaxation as you allow yourself to relax even more. Now allow that same deep state of relaxation that you have within your eyelids to continue to float down over the rest of your body, knowing that you are doing wonderfully.

This is a very special time that you are devoting to yourself, to give yourself the opportunity to learn and explore the magnificence within you. You may already intimately know the power and abilities that lie deep within you, or perhaps you have a thought or idea of what they could be and have felt them from time to time, or maybe you are simply hopeful to find the true you that you've always known was there. Whichever it is for you, the truth is that you are more amazing than you give yourself credit for.

Now as you continue to relax even more deeply, not caring exactly how you are causing the relaxation within your body, only knowing it is happening much more quickly and easily than you thought possible, in your mind's eye and in your imagination, notice a pair of elevator doors. This is your very safe custom elevator. As you notice all the details of the doors, see these doors slowly open. Enter your elevator and look around. Notice the interior: the walls, the ceiling, the floor, the lighting. Make sure everything is exactly as you would choose it to be. Now close the doors and we'll go down to a special, beautiful place deep within your subconscious mind.

If you're ready, and you'd like to, we can get started now.

Notice you are on the 25th floor. With each floor you pass you will go deeper into relaxation and inward focus. If you are ready, the elevator is starting to go down from 25... relaxing and letting go, 24, 23, sinking into a comfortable, calm, peaceful position, 22 feeling safe and secure, 21, 20, 19, going down into deeper relaxation, 18, 17, 16, knowing that the deeper you go, the better you feel; and the better you feel, the deeper you go, 15, going down, 14, and down, 13, and down, 12, 11, 10, letting go, 9, 8, way down deep, 7, deeper and deeper, 6, 5, 4, knowing that the deeper you go the better you feel, 3, 2, feeling so good, and finally, 1, the doors open and you step out into your favorite place in nature.

In front of you there is a large clear plastic bag. As you look at the bag notice many things about it, especially the clarity with which you can see through the bag to the inside. You can see very clearly what is in this bag.

One thing you notice right away is the color inside of the bag, a beautiful purple swirling color, slowly moving around in the bag, almost iridescent. Just for a moment watch the purple light swirling slowly inside the bag.

There are some things that you can place in the bag, if you like. Some things about yourself, your thoughts your ideas, your difficulties, your hopes...

Begin by putting into the bag your name and everything it means about you; what it says about you, how it feels to have this name. Notice it just swirling in the purple light.

Place in the bag your clothes; your favorite outfit; your entire wardrobe.

Place in the bag your hairstyle, and your makeup. Notice what it says about you, what kind of statement it makes, what it means about you.

Watch it all slowly swirling in the bag. Notice those things that are important to you.

Put in the bag your furniture; your entire house; everything in it.

Notice all of those things you own, swirling in the purple mist.

Now in the bag put your car; what it says about you; what you are trying to tell people about yourself.

Now put your phone in the bag. All of your possessions in the bag. Put your job in the bag, and all those ideas that you are what you do...

Put in the bag your mind, and with it that little voice in the back of your mind that is always telling you what to think and what to do.

Put your personality in the bag; your dreams, your nightmares...

place in the bag your beliefs all of your beliefs about money, men, women, sex, your sex organs, beliefs about your weight, your complexion; beliefs about race, God, religion, politics.

Place in the bag all of the ideas and fears you have about death and loneliness.

Put your mother in the bag, and all of your ideas and thoughts about her.

Put your father in the bag.

In the bag now place your sisters, brothers, grandparents, husband or wife, children, friends.

Put in the bag anyone you have ever hurt, anyone who has hurt you.

Put all of your complaints in the bag, anything you have ever complained about...

All your judgments in the bag. Those people and things you felt were good, bad, right, wrong.

Put in the bag your need to always be right. Your opinions, opinions about what you have and have not accomplished; opinions about failure, reputation, things you're guilty of, laws you broke, arguments you had.

Put in the bag all the agreements you didn't keep. All the relationships you left, all the relationships that left you. Put in the bag opinions others have about you; opinions your parents had about what they wanted you to be, what your friends wanted you to be, what your boss wanted you to be.

Put in the bag what your enemies think of you.

Your characteristics, habits, addictions, your resistance, put it all in the bag, and just watch it all swirling and moving; all those things that are you, that define you.

Put in the bag your need to be argumentative or revengeful, your need to be alone, your desire to not tell the truth, your desire to not confront others.

Put in the bag your refusal to let other people teach you, your reluctance to empower other people...

In the bag put all of your fears. Your need to justify what you do wrong, the reasons for why you are what you are.

Put all of your current problems in the bag. All of those things about you; swirling in the bag in the purple misty light.

Now, look around and put anything you might have forgotten in the bag; anything about you, put it all in there. Everything that is you is in the bag.

Now put your clothes you are wearing in the bag. Put your naked body in the bag. See everything that is you, in the bag, all swirling around in the bag, with the purple light.

But, you are not in the bag. You are who is looking at the bag. You created everything in that bag to help you experience yourself.

You can keep or discard anything in the bag, it is your choice. It is your choice. It is not you. You are not who is in the bag. You are not the things in the bag. You are who is looking at the bag.

Now you can keep whatever you choose, it is your choice. In a moment, you are going to give the bag a big kick. You are going to send that bag into the universe, far away from here and let it go.

Ready? Now when I count to three, give it a big kick; so hard that is goes flying far into the outer reaches of the universe. Ready? One, two, three, and watch it go, farther and farther away; so far that is gets really small, now becoming a tiny speck in the distance, so small now that it is totally gone. Just gone.

Now all that remains is the true and magnificent you. This is the REAL you. This is all that matters. Notice the peace and calm within all parts of your mind, body, and spirit. Hear the delicate yet powerful silence that emanates from you. Feel the clarity you are experiencing in this present moment where nothing else matters. You simply are... completely whole... so light and free.

You are the breath of the universe. You are the creation. You are the creator. You are consciousness. You are awareness. You are abundant, prosperous, magnificent. You are love. You are beauty. You are inspiration. You are joy and happiness. You are the stillness. You are the truth. You are spirit. You are Divine. You are life. You are a seed of the Great I Am.

Know in the very depths of your innermost being that your life truly is of your own creation. Today you can decide for the rest of your life, exactly how you choose your life to be. Welcoming into your life only those things that are in your best interest. And embracing the health, happiness, and abundance that are within you always. Treasuring the sweetness of each and every moment that comes to you, as you live each day to the fullest, experiencing how truly amazing you are.

As your subconscious mind and all levels of your inner mind are now memorizing this truth and awareness, you find it easy to take with you all that you have learned. Allowing this wisdom to influence your thoughts, feelings, and actions from this moment forward as you create your best life possible.

Take a nice deep breath, bring your awareness back your surroundings, and open your eyes.

INFINITE

"Infinite Possibilities.. What Will I Choose?"

The world has conspired since the beginning of time to create you. There could be no other. Cosmic forces came together and in an instant you were here. From nowhere to here. A spark of the Divine manifested into form to experience Itself in all Its glory.

You come from an infinite source of all that is creative, loving, good, abundant, and everlasting. You are here now being human, yet it doesn't diminish your essence. Your task is simply to find the place within where you can allow those Divine qualities to shine through brightly.

Paramahansa Yogananda taught us to "know that this universe is nothing but a dream bluff of nature to test your consciousness of immortality." The children's rhyme song Row, Row, Row Your Boat reminds us that life is but a dream. The world we perceive is an illusion we each create with our minds.

Being born a human being, not only do you contain within you the infinite wisdom of millions of people who have come before you, but you hold within the infinite wisdom of your own true infinite Self. Your deepest Self brought you to the place where you are in this very moment, closer to the place of remembrance. You are on a path of rediscovery so that you may uncover and expand the truth of who you are and the world in which you live.

Through endless time and space, you move. Through many states of consciousness and understanding, you are witness to the unfolding of creation – yours and the Universe itself – all deriving from the single source of infinite possibilities.

This visualization exercise will allow you to remember that in every moment there is an infinite number of possibilities from which you may choose, and to actively choose those things that move you toward where you want to go.

VISUALIZATION - FLYING WITH FAIRIES

*T*ake a deep breath. Let the world around you begin to melt and disappear. Let every breath you breathe fill you with a sense of peace and comfort. Let your every exhale release any tension or tightness. In this moment, right here, right now, just allow yourself to breathe softly and gently. Inhale. Exhale. Just breathe.

In your mind's eye and in your imagination, find yourself walking along a path. It is a smooth dirt path that leads to the most beautiful and inviting forest you could imagine. It has a magical glow about it that sparkles with intrigue and mystery.

Moving forward at a comfortable speed you soon draw near. Before you at the entrance of the forest, there is a table. Upon that table there is a jar that is filled with an iridescent glistening substance that is not quite solid, not quite liquid. It is as if it hasn't yet finished coming into form. Yet it is clear that it is meant for you, and only you, to walk upon this path, and take a pinch between your fingers, and travel this journey.

As you do, the magical jar shimmers and out from the

forest fly beautiful winged beings that seem to be fairies of some sort, here to be with you as you venture forward.

They somehow gift you with the ability to move with them and together you effortlessly glide into the forest. Yet they allow you to take the lead on this journey to what you seek. The forest is alive with wisdom and guidance in every form. It is filled with infinite possibilities, with each choice, and every path, leading you in a different direction.

In your heart, you know which way you should go. It may not always be the easiest way or may require more effort, but if you listen closely you can hear it calling you, guiding you in the direction that is for your best and highest good.

The path you find yourself upon is new yet familiar somehow. It has all the familiar sights and sounds you have grown accustomed to. It feels comfortable and predictable. Over time, the colors begin to lose their luster and the things that once uplifted and filled you with joy now no longer have that same effect. You recognize you could continue, but at some point, you come to a fork in the path.

One path, the path you have been on, continues down and to the left. You sense the fairies waiting there with you, beside you, holding a loving space of support and encouragement. You intuitively know you are never alone. As you look at the familiar path, the colors are somewhat dull and you begin to notice a slight heaviness about it. Still, you wonder if it is the path that will lead you to your desires.

The other path continues up and to the right. This is a new and unfamiliar path you have not yet explored. There is a certain brightness to it and you sense within a feeling of energy, curiosity, and eagerness about the possibilities of what may lie ahead. You wonder how this path will lead you to your goals.

You make your choice once you notice yourself focusing on one path more than the other. You feel a sense of certainty within that you have chosen the best path for yourself in this moment.

As you travel upon this path, you develop new thoughts and ideas that lead you to another choice point. You tune your attention inward and get that same sensation, that same sense of knowing or certainty that shows you which way to go.

Moving forward you begin to understand that you are lovingly being guided from within and those surrounding you. Yet your choices are always yours, and the world around you bends to those choices you make. With this awareness, you are gently lifted to a higher perspective. Here you discover that there are an infinite number of choices and possibilities. You understand there are no wrong choices, as every path ultimately leads you to your true purpose. Some paths may wind and twist in unexpected ways, while others meander this way and that. Some are more direct, some require more effort, yet every single choice is an opportunity to learn and shift and grow into a more pure version of who you truly are.

You feel yourself relax more deeply into your journey here in this place. You see yourself absorbing this wisdom and notice yourself trusting your internal guidance and the guidance around you. You know the mystical, the magical, and Divine energy surrounds, comforts, and uplifts you always. You have such peace and ease, trusting and knowing your future is of your own creation and every step forward brings you closer to your goals.

Breathe in deeply, exhale, and carry this wisdom forward with you.

JUST ASK

"The Moment I Ask, I Know It's on Its Way"

Folk talks and folk lore are filled with stories of magical genies in lamps, elves in trees, guardians, and wish masters that grant your wishes, but they are often fraught with limitations, restrictions, and consequences. There may be some caveat or loophole in which your requests need not be fulfilled, or the manner in which you receive them are not the outcome you intended. There is frequently a price of some sort to be paid in exchange for asking your wishes. These stories often teach you to have gratitude for the life and things you already have, before you ask for something more or different.

Yet so often you can feel as if the things you long for are doomed to remain just a daydream or wishful thinking. You do not fully believe that it is possible, or that you are deserving, worthy, or capable of having your dreams come true. You have forgotten who you are and where you come from. The apple does not fall far from the tree. Manifesting begins with your asking. What you ask for and believe in your heart as already yours, will show up in your reality in a matter of time.

Your asking activates the lawful guiding principles of the Universe. There is nothing in this world you can ask for that is impossible for you to achieve. Everything is available to you in this moment for asking. The only way you can become a co-creator in your life is to ask for the things you desire. Ask with clear intention and the faith and belief that the Universe is shaping itself to accommodate your desires.

The Bible says, "Ask and it will be given to you; seek and you will find; knock and it shall be opened unto you." Your wish is the Universal command.

Asking is how you communicate your desires. Mother Meera taught to "Ask for everything - like a child asks its mother for everything, without shame. Do not stop at peace of mind or purity of heart or surrender. Demand everything. Don't be satisfied with anything less than everything. If you ask, you will receive."

Ask for help from someone who has traveled the path before you. Ask for help from someone who can guide you. Ask for help from the source of everything so It can rise up and offer what you need. It starts with you asking, then believing.

This visualization exercise will allow you to step into the mind of someone who has what it is you would like for yourself. It will give you an opportunity to experience what it is like to feel, be, and experience everything from the perspective that your desires are something you have already achieved, so you can more fully embrace those same thoughts, feelings, and beliefs as your own.

VISUALIZATION - GENIUS MIND

*T*ake a nice big deep breath, and as you exhale, allow yourself to settle into a comfortable position. As you take another deep breath and allow yourself to begin to relax, in your mind's eye and in your imagination, notice before you is a magical door... you might imagine it, see it, feel it, or just simply know it's there. In a moment you're going to open the door and step through, and when you do, it will take you into any time and any place... taking you into a magical world to experience the possibilities of what lies within you.

In this magical world, you will be able to step into the mind of a genius and experience what it is like to have infinite confidence and wisdom. To feel the success, the freedom, the abilities. To see how it shapes your thoughts, feelings, and beliefs. To hear others sharing in your joy and accomplishments. To learn the secrets of a genius' success. To learn and understand that you have the same potential within you.

On the count of three, when you go through that door, you will allow your mind to go into a very deep and pleasant state within as you focus on my voice and allow my voice to guide you. Immersing yourself into this wonderful magical world where all things are possible... all things are within reach.

Ready... feeling the excitement and curiosity building within you... one... two... three. Open the door and go through... and you enter a magical world filled with unending secrets. You can sense there is great wisdom here. Wisdom waiting to be shared...with you.

Begin to notice all the details of this place. The more you focus on the details, the clearer they become. Moving toward you is the genius who will teach you everything you need to know at this moment in time. You can see the confidence and self-assurance this genius possesses. Knowledge and wisdom seem to radiate from this being, and you can feel the energy as you have now come face to face.

As you look into the eyes of this genius, you sense an expression of knowingness... remembering what it was like to be where you are now. Re-experiencing the learnings and lessons necessary to achieve greatness. You feel its kindness and generosity beaming in all directions. You trust that you will find the answers you are seeking.

Right now, ask your genius what you need to know at this moment in time... to move forward... to become even more wise and intelligent... and then listen to the response. Your inner mind recognizes the first thought, feeling, or sensation you receive as an answer to your question.

Perhaps this genius knows something you have been doing to limit yourself, or maybe even what you should focus your attention on. So ask your genius, "What is the most important thing for me to learn, understand, and incorporate into my life in order to bring forward incredible wisdom and abilities?" And then wait for the answer.

If you need further clarification, ask your genius to give you more details so that you can truly succeed. (pause)

Knowing you wish to learn even more, and willing to share everything with you, the genius nods its head granting permission to step inside the being's mind and body, and experience everything about this genius, from the inside out.

You allow yourself to step inside that body... you are now in this genius. The first thing you become intimately aware of is the calm and confidence permeating every muscle, cell, and fiber of your genius. Notice the overwhelming sense of peace that has removed all static and interference that once was there, and feel how good it is to be relaxed and at ease. All body processes are relaxed and free flowing. Body and mind are in perfect harmony and balance.

Notice your outlook on the world... how things seem easier and more manageable. The world is simpler, more enjoyable, and exciting. Listen to your inner thoughts... all you can hear are the positive attributes of yourself and others.

Become aware of the infinite knowledge and wisdom of this genius. Sense the skills and abilities that have developed.

Discover how good it feels to have this confidence and wisdom.

Notice what it is that you have done to achieve this greatness. Find something to show you how you got to this point... where learning and understanding became easy and enjoyable. Perhaps find a routine or a way to absorb and understand information quickly and easily.

Now on the count of three, step out of your genius so that you are once again face to face. 1, 2, 3, good. As you look into the eyes of your genius, feel grateful for everything your genius has shared with you. Send a wave of appreciation down over your entire body, and find a way to allow this information to resonate deep within every part of your mind, body, and spirit. Knowing that some of the information is conscious, and other information is deep within your mind... soon to be discovered.

Now, bring your attention back to the room in the here and now. Bring with you the lessons and learnings of your time spent with your genius. Beginning now, and in the next few days, you will discover yourself experiencing new thoughts, feelings, and beliefs about yourself and your abilities. Your time spent in this magical world has taught you that you are not that different from your genius. All things are possible... all things are within your reach. You must only believe in yourself, and you will find that the magic is all around you... and the magic is within you.

PLANT SEEDS

"Today's Thoughts Become Tomorrow's Garden"

It is your inherent divine right to fulfill the greatest expression of your full potential. Within you lies all the seeds of your grandeur, encased with infinite possibilities to make them bloom and prosper. You are the master gardener designing the landscape of your life.

It is up to you to create the blueprint that will yield the most perfect arrangement and embodiment of all that you can be. Every seed, every thought, matters. Every open space left vacant will be filled with intention or by default.

Your results are often not immediate; germinating in the medium of the divine until the moment the conditions are right for their appearance and arrival.

With the proper attention, care, and nurturance, the seeds become what they were created to be. Yet they still require vigilance to ensure they remain viable and hardy, able to withstand the outside factors and influences that may attempt to challenge or threaten them until they are strong enough to exist on their own.

You will reap what you sow. You can choose to be all that you are or you can choose to be less. Whichever seeds you choose will become your experience tomorrow. By staying true to who you are, embracing your gifts and talents, and everything that is you, you will create a future where only good and kindness follow you for all the days of your life. Very soon you will feel the ripple as you feel the touch of your impact from the outside.

Allow this visualization to remind you of the power you hold within yourself. The fertile seeds of thought possess the future. Find the seeds that are best suited to flower into your goals and dreams.

VISUALIZATION - POT OF GOLD

*C*lose your eyes. Take a deep breath. Let your body and mind begin to relax. Let your arms relax, let your shoulders relax, and just allow all the muscles in your body to begin to soften and release their hold. As your body and mind continue to relax, allow your mind to drift into a peaceful place within where you are comfortable, safe, and at ease.

In your mind's eye, imagine that you have found yourself immersed in the heart of the storm. You look around and take in the scene, noticing all the details. As you look to the sky, you notice that the sun is hidden behind the clouds. And in the darkness, you can sense the heaviness of the raindrops, as the clouds seem to release and let go. The little hairs covering your body begin to rise, as the cool, damp surroundings somehow surround you. And the wind... blowing and whistling strongly from the west... pushes against you with all of its might. But you stand strong and firm. You look down to your feet and notice the ground below you is a rough, uneven, and winding dirt road. And you are struck by the power of the scene... but deep within yourself, you possess a knowingness that you can walk quickly and surely through... never to return.

Where obstacles once would have stopped you or slowed you down, you begin to move forward through the storm, and before you know it, as you move forward along the path, the skies lighten... the clouds dissipate... and the day turns into the most beautiful summer's day you can imagine. The warmth of the sun creates the perfect temperature. You look up and the sky is the bluest blue you have ever seen. Not a cloud in the sky as far as the eye can see. You notice an arching rainbow – the colors so alive and beautiful – whose end lies off in the distance. And you wonder what it would be like to find the pot of gold at the end of the rainbow, and have all your hopes, wishes, goals, and dreams come true. As you think about the possibilities, you feel an ever so slight warm breeze caressing your body into complete relaxation, peace, and harmony. And the wind carries with it a pure and sweet fragrance from the nearby flowers. You breathe in deeply and feel calm and relaxed, loving the space you are in. You become aware of the animals returning to normal activity now that the storm has passed. You hear the birds signing their summer melody. All traces of the storm are now gone.

And as you move along the path, now a smooth paved path, you come upon a large, open field. It seems to have a magical golden glow about it. You bend down and take a scoop of the virgin soil into your hands. The soil is a deep, rich, healthy color, full of minerals and nutrients... ready and waiting to be planted with seeds that will quickly bloom and prosper.

You reach into your pocket and find a full bag of healthy seeds... seeds filled with your hopes, wishes, goals, and dreams. They have been with you your entire journey, and yet, you were unaware that you had carried them with you. You open the bag, and find the seeds of hopes, wishes, goals, and dreams you want to see bloom into being. In another pocket, you find you carry all of the necessary tools in order to plant your seeds... these too, are always with you.

You begin planting your seeds... one by one. Taking time to think about each one as you lovingly place it into the healthy and rich soil. As you continue planting your seeds, you notice the colors of the rainbow shining down directly onto your field. And you think back to the time just after the storm... when you first saw the rainbow and wondered what it would be like to find the pot of gold at the end of the rainbow, where all your wishes, hopes, and dreams would come true. And here you are. You wonder how you could have not seen the beautiful colors shining down on you and this fertile field... where you continue to plant your seeds. Knowing without a doubt... that you have found the end of the rainbow, and your pot of gold where all your hopes, wishes, goals, and dreams will come true.

Your future is now clearly of your own creation. You hold the seeds of all your hopes, wishes, goals, and dreams... and as you move forward in the realization that you can create the kind of life you are seeking, each and every moment it becomes easier and clearer in your mind what you need to do to achieve it.

RELAX

"*Relax and Enjoy the Gifts of Life*"

Life can be complex.

Whether with permission or by force, the external world often places demands upon you that you can feel obligated to fulfill. In addition, you have your own demands and expectations that you have placed upon yourself in order to feel satisfied and content. Sometimes the expectations can become unrealistic and life no longer is a joy.

It can be easy to get caught up in the busyness of life. Without awareness, you can mistakenly allow your self-worth to become entangled in the outcomes of these tasks. Regardless of the results experienced, who you are will never change. You are a Divine being experiencing all aspects of life. Each experience is an opportunity to reconnect with your inner self, through the vessels of a variety of situations.

You can give yourself permission to soften your expectations while striving for the things you desire in life. It is all unfolding in the most perfect way.

In Tilopa's Six Words of Advice teaching, he tells us to "Let go of what has passed. Let go of what may come. Let go of what is happening now. Don't try to figure anything out. Don't try to make anything happen. Relax, right now, and rest."

Now is a time set aside just for you, so you can allow yourself to relax and let go, and focus only upon yourself for a few moments. If you have any cares or worries, you can simply let them fade and disappear. If any are important to you, if you choose, they can be there when your quiet time is through, but for now, give yourself permission to just relax and let go.

This visualization exercise will allow you to calm yourself and go within to that place where you can truly be at ease and connect with your inner self. In this place, you can discover more than physical relaxation. You can discover an connection to the gifts that life has given you.

VISUALIZATION - RAINBOW STEPS

*T*ake a nice big deep breath, and as you exhale, allow yourself to settle into a comfortable position. As you take another deep breath and allow yourself to begin to relax, in your mind's eye and in your imagination, take yourself to the top of a set of steps.

They are the most extraordinarily colorful steps you can possibly imagine. As you look down the steps, it's almost as though you are looking down a rainbow that leads to a wonderfully relaxing and most inviting bed that reminds you of a soft white fluffy cloud. As you look at it you realize you want to be there.

You want to be in that beautiful bed and allow its magic to take you to the most peaceful place within yourself. That wonderful place where everything just feels right. Where you can set aside any thoughts or cares or worries of the day. That place where you can just relax into all that is.

As you look down these rainbow steps, you understand that every shade of every color is here in this rainbow of steps before you... inviting you forward into both the soft and the bold and all those spaces in between. And you intuitively know that each step will take you deeper into this wonderful relaxation and deeper within, until... at last... you effortlessly sink into this deep and restful state of deep relaxation within.

And so you take the first step. The first step is the color of red, and as you step onto it, you become filled with the color of red. The color of red permeates every cell of your being from the tips of your toes to the tip of your nose. Every shade of red can be felt on this step as you hear the color of red.

Red, red, red.

Red like the color of a fragrant rose, red like the color of a ladybug, red like the color of a cardinal's feathers. The color of a deliciously ripe strawberry, apple, or the inside of a watermelon. The color of love that fills your heart with safety and security and the feeling that everything is as it should be, and that all shall be well.

And you feel comforted by the color of red. You become red, and you are red.

As your color red begins to shine more brightly, you take the next step onto the color of orange. And as you step onto this step you become filled with the color of orange. The color of orange moves up your body until every cell of your being overflows with orange, filling every muscle, every fiber, every nerve, and every cell of your being with the color and character of orange.

Orange, orange, orange.

Orange like the orange fruit, and the orange of a peach, a pumpkin, and a carrot. The orange of a goldfish serenely swimming and the soft orange glow of a warm fire. The sunset orange at the end of the day reminding you of the beauty and serenity all around you. The warm color of creativity and change that whispers of your vitality and strength in this space of peace, trust, surrender, and deep wisdom.

And you feel comforted by the color of orange and the joy it brings. You become orange, and you are orange.

As your color orange begins to radiate within more strongly, you take the next step onto the color of yellow. And as you step onto this step you become filled with the color of yellow. The color of yellow tingles the soles of your feet as you step into your personal power and become filled with a deep sense of confidence and conviction in knowing exactly who you are.

Yellow, yellow, yellow.

Yellow brings the innocence of a yellow rubber duck and a soft fluffy chick. And the yellow of a daffodil and a dandelion sharing their gifts. The vital yellow of the sun that sustains and provides for you. The yellow of a canary, a banana, and a lemon. Beautiful shades of yellow shining within.

And you feel comforted by the color of yellow. You become yellow, and you are yellow.

As the energy of yellow flows freely within, you feel yourself connecting deeply and authentically to your inner self as you choose to move forward with self-love, value, and worth onto the next step as you continue relaxing into the colors with each and every breath you take and with each and every color you experience. And the next step is the color of green. The lovely color of green that resonates within your heart as it too moves up your body in the most beautifully gentle and compassionate way.

Green, green, green.

Green as the grass, and the leaves on the trees. The green of a four-leaf clover, and the green of a frog and a lizard. Green like a grape, an avocado, a kiwi, and a lime. The green of an emerald that is truly sublime.

As the color of green grows within you feel love and warmth and healing. You become filled with kindness and compassion for yourself and others, knowing the truth that you are part of something bigger than what you see before you. You feel yourself spreading this love and deep connection with others through every motion you make.

And you feel comforted by the color of green. You become green, and you are green.

As your color green begins to shine more brightly, you take the next step onto the color of blue. And as you step onto this step you become filled with the color of blue. The color of blue moves up through your body in the most beautifully sacred way allowing all parts of your being to see, hear, and feel the color and character of blue.

Blue, blue, blue.

The blue of a summer sky. The blue of your favorite jeans that fit just right. The bluest blue water that you have ever seen. The blue like a blueberry and a sapphire. Blue like a bluebird that sings its song for all to hear. Blue speaks to you of embracing your uniqueness and speaking your truth. Blue allows you to see your gifts, the guidance, and the deep meanings and understanding that is here for you.

And you feel comforted by the color of blue. You become blue, and you are blue.

As your color blue begins to settle within, you take the next step onto the color of purple. And as you step onto this step you become filled with the color of purple. The color of purple shines forth from your bottom all the way through your top and you feel a deep sense of gratitude, joy, and trust.

Purple, purple, purple.

Purple like a plum, a grape, and an eggplant. The deep purple of a night sky. The purple of lilac and amethyst.

And you feel comforted by the royal color of purple. You become purple, and you are purple. Purple fills you with a knowing that you are divinely guided from within and from without. That there is nothing to do but to love, and to trust, and to be... completely at ease with yourself and the world around you.

And so, at last, you can allow yourself to take that last and most peaceful step into the soft and weightless white that beckons you. The white that surrounds you like a warm blanket and wraps you up in peace, comfort, and stillness. In this white bed, you allow yourself to slumber in wholeness, purity, and truth... awakening to your deepest self in your own time... at your own pace.

And when you are ready, you may return your awareness back to your surroundings and awaken.

SIMPLICITY

" *To See a World in a Grain of Sand...*"

All things in the Universe are interconnected. Every minute detail is interwoven into the very fabric of all there is, was, and will be. Each are interwoven into the details of the whole, each significant in its own uniqueness, vital to the outcome. It is a complex simplicity which surrounds you. Anything is everything. It is beckoning you to take notice, to pay attention.

Yet often you can get caught up in too many of the specific details. When you allow your focus to become too narrowed, you risk losing perspective of the whole. A step back will allow you to see the beauty of the details in motion, in their simplicity.

William Blake's poem eloquently demonstrates this: "To see a world in a grain of sand and heaven in a wild flower, hold infinity in the palm of your hand and eternity in an hour."

To understand the wisdom and intelligence behind each detail, when viewed as a whole, is to understand. Everything is important, and yet it is not important to understand everything. And so it is with your own journey, your own process. The details of your own life, too, possess this complex simplicity. All the details in your life demonstrate the perfection that life is as it should be.

This visualization exercise will allow you to remember that every detail, every opportunity, and every situation, is a part of the universal precision that is occurring for the Universe to unfold itself to meet your requests. It is your choice whether or not to see them as such.

VISUALIZATION - BURIED TREASURES

*T*ake a deep breath, and as you exhale, allow yourself to get a little more comfortable and a little more relaxed. Let go of any tension or tightness in your neck or shoulders, and notice the way your eyes feel right now. Allow your eyelids to get heavy, loose, and relaxed.

Perhaps you'd like to close your eyes right now or maybe you would like to in a few moments when it feels just right for you... knowing there is nothing you need to do, nowhere for you to be, nobody is wanting anything from you, nobody is expecting anything from you.

So you can just allow yourself to perhaps become aware of the sounds around you, and you can allow those sounds to begin to relax you. Allow those sounds to float in and out of your awareness, and allow the muscles of your body to relax so deeply and completely, as you become more relaxed than you could possibly imagine.

Let your body breathe so very softly, gently. Notice that each breath effortlessly floats in and then out of your body, and every time you exhale you relax into those sounds around you, breathing so easily, softly, slowly. Anytime you'd like to

relax deeper, you take a breath, and as you exhale you go even deeper within into that perfect and peaceful place of home.

As you allow your mind and body to relax so deeply, in the velvety darkness behind your eyes, notice yourself standing on a boardwalk...it is a boardwalk that has been aged with time. Yet its strength and beauty remain, heightened actually. A gentle breeze softly ruffles the sea oats beside you as you journey along the path. You smell the salty air before your eyes hold the vision of vastness before them. Seagulls fly overhead as your feet carry you to the shore. You feel your body settle into a calmer pace when you are here. You feel yourself relax in the deep places you didn't even realize you had held tension. It's as though you had, in a sense, been holding your breath, and now you are finally able to breathe deeply.

You allow yourself to just Be... in the moment... with no expectations, no agenda. Just a silent witness to the beauty before, around, and taking place within you. You notice a bird flying freely overhead and imagine yourself soaring with the same grace and ease. As you are observing the bird, it plunges deep into the water. After a moment or two it surfaces with a treasure that will nourish itself and allow it to grow and thrive.

Your gaze shifts to the sandpipers running along the shore. Confidently and with great certainty they rush in where opportunity awaits them between the waves. They do not linger but have faith they will find an abundance of what they seek. They watch the signs that guide them, trusting in the wisdom within and without.

As the waves roll in you notice the shells that ebb and flow with the rhythm of universe. Some land at your feet and are easy to reach down and grab. Others have only partially revealed themselves or leave just as quickly as they came. Still others swirl around, require more effort, and are a bit more challenging. And you understand it is always your choice in what to pursue. The waves of the world give, and the waves wash away. Their gifts are never lost, they just move on.

You allow yourself to step more deeply in, allowing the waves in this very moment to flow to you, full of their peace and their treasures being offered to you. And as it always does, the waves cleanse and wash, renewing that which it surrounds. The ever-present pull of the universe moves the deep places within you and in this very moment, all is well. In this very moment, you are a part of something much greater than yourself, and yet you are the orchestrator as you step and dance and flow with the rhythm in the way that is uniquely yours.

And you breathe it in and let yourself be.

All is well. All is well. All is well.

SPIRIT

"*Spirit Move Me*"

The spirit or consciousness of the Universe is omnipresent. There is nowhere it is not, and as such, this spirit dwells within you. It is that quiet voice inside you that whispers its guidance. It is the true you that resides within your physical body.

That you are more than a physical being, but rather a spiritual being having a physical experience, is never more apparent than when you witness someone crossing over to the next place.

If you have ever held the space around a loved one as they are dying, perhaps you have felt it. If you give yourself permission to experience this opportunity, in the moment without anything attached to it, the sacredness of what is happening can be breathtakingly beautiful. It can be a reminder to yourself of the spirit that is within you.

This has been my experience. Stillness surrounds them as

it surrounds you. The air becomes thick with only pure love. Nothing else matters in that moment in time. You become fully present. History has no meaning. Yet you become profoundly aware that your life will forever be changed. Nothing can ever return to the way it was; and maybe that is a blessing. Perhaps it is as if this is the last gift this person has given you, as you witness their transition.

In the hours or moments leading up to their last breath, this special gift they have offered to you is actually a threefold expression of mind, body and spirit.

If you are fortunate, you have the gift of sharing with them everything you need to while you can still look at, touch, and hold their body. You have the opportunity to make peace with them and yourself.

Even deeper than that, you can see the beauty of the human body and recognize its magnificence. During life, everything works without effort. It is the temple in which we house our most sacred Self. You would do well to treat it with kindness, gratitude, and love, as it deserves nothing less.

Still even deeper than that, at the moment of their crossing stillness surrounds their body in a way that nothing else on earth can. You are greeted with the fact that this person's essence, their spirit, is no longer within their body. The recognition that you are more than your body, and all that it may seem to be, becomes ever present. If you remain open to clues around you perhaps you will experience your loved one in a different form, in such a way that you can be sure it could only be them. Your spirit lies within your body until that moment when it moves on to somewhere else. Where that somewhere else is you may never know until it is your time to exhale this life and inhale your new life. The truth of this last gift you have been given is the knowledge that, in the purest sense of the word, you will never die. Chapter 2 verse 5 of Colossians in the Holy Bible reminds us that "For though I be absent in the flesh, yet am I with you in the spirit."

For in the impending emotions that may come lies an opportunity for deep inner reflection. This is the type of reflection that would not have occurred unless something as monumental as physically losing someone does. In the stillness before, during, and after someone's crossing you can feel the pulse of God as you witness one person's transition through your many forms.

Philosopher Rumi declared, "When I die I will soar with angels. What I shall become You cannot imagine." We become, or perhaps more fully embrace, more of what we have always been. "Why should I seek?" he says. "I am the same as He. His essence speaks through me. I have been looking for myself!"

This visualization exercise will allow you to internalize how you truly are a spiritual being having a physical experience.

VISUALIZATION - BRIDGE TO BEYOND

*I*t has been said that there is a bridge you must cross when you transition from one life and into the next. All cultures throughout the ages have identified with an afterlife in various forms. You are now remembering what you have always known. You are a spiritual being.

In the next few moments, you will have an opportunity to reconnect with a loved one who has transitioned from this life. It will be an opportunity for you to give yourself a gift of healing, connection, or re-experiencing your deep love. It will be a positive and uplifting experience that will help you move forward and grow.

Take a deep breath, and as you let it out, allow yourself to begin to connect to that place within you where you feel your love the strongest. It is a place within that can never empty, but only fill and be filled because love is your essence. It is who you are and it has no edges or boundaries.

Take yourself there in your mind's eye, to that place of pure and deep love where nothing else matters. In that place, as your body and mind continue to relax, discover yourself in a field. It is a beautiful field that makes you feel very peaceful and secure. It is somehow familiar in a curious way, as you feel as though you have been here before, in every part of this field.

Your eyes notice a beautiful bridge leading to another area that is also beautiful yet has some sort of mist or haziness to it that you can't quite see beyond. It feels pleasant and inviting and also familiar, yet you sense it is not your time to cross over the bridge to the other side.

Notice a large white cushy chair near the bridge. You know exactly how to get to it. Sit in the chair. As you relax, you allow your heart and mind to fill with thoughts and memories of a loved one. You sense the moments with this loved one that shaped your life. You feel how they impacted your growth and outlook in life.

As you are remembering this loved one, you notice a movement from upon the bridge. Your loved one has felt your love, heard as a calling to them, and has joined with you here in this moment.

You feel an intimate closeness with them in your heart, body, and mind and it is as if time and space have disappeared, and you are together once again. You take a deep breath, and as you let it out, you feel yourself relax more deeply and peacefully than you have in quite some time. They feel your love, and you feel their love for you in every part of your mind, body, and spirit.

In this quiet moment between you, allow yourself to share everything you need to share with them. All of your thoughts and feelings that you need to communicate with them, they willingly and lovingly receive.

Hear the words and sounds you need to hear from them as they share the love they have for you. Feel their embrace.

Ask them if they have a special message for you to help you grow or move forward in the way that is for your best and highest good. Then listen deeply with all parts of your mind, body, and spirit so that you understand exactly the meaning of this message.

If you need further clarification, ask them for more information. They are here to love and support you in whatever way you most need.

Know that they are here for you whenever you need them; to talk to, to listen to, to just be with each other.

Allow your loved one to travel back over the bridge, and experience them in the misty love that surrounds them. They are at peace.

You know that you can return to this place, to this white chair, at any time in the future. Whenever you come here, you will always get exactly what you need in that moment for your best and highest good.

Take a deep breath in, feel the love for you and them. Bring that love forward with you now and always.

STILLNESS

"In Stillness I Feel the Pulse of God"

There is an indescribable stillness and consciousness that underlies the Universe. It is the guiding force within and without that is accessible to you in every moment.

It is peace, and power, and purpose. It is wisdom, and awareness, and potentiality. It is silence, and serenity, and pure bliss. It is everything and it is nothing; both existing in the same space without time.

It is a stillness so palpable you know it could be nothing other than the pulse of the Universe itself; the place your deepest Self calls home.

Most often, it is a stillness that you must consciously seek and make time to discover. A spontaneous connection and awareness of this stillness may occur, although for most people, it is experienced through dedicated practice or through a trauma of some sort.

You know it when you are there, in the gap between

everything. In the stillness, you simply are. You are more than yourself. You move beyond who you think you are and sink into all that you are. An old proverb tells us, "No one can see their reflection in running water. It is only in still water that we can see."

You become awareness and the breath of life. In the quiet, you stop your exploration having arrived at the place you started, as T.S. Eliot shared, and know it for the first time. You must go within. It is there you will find respite. Your hidden wholeness lies just beneath this outer world.

Deep within you lies all of the answers to all of your questions. In moments of silence and stillness you expand your awareness to this inner knowledge, and the path before you becomes clear. Give yourself permission to experience all that your life can be and embrace your infinite wisdom. You already know how to do it.

This visualization exercise will allow you to connect to that silent and still place within that is filled with peace and calm, where you become everything and nothing at the same time.

VISUALIZATION - THE GLOW

$\mathcal{T}$ake a deep breath in. Exhale and relax. With intention, allow yourself to set aside the world outside. It will be there for you when you return. With your next breath, silently say to yourself, "Peace." With your next exhalation, silently say to yourself, "Calm." Breathe in, peace. Breathe out, calm. Peace. Calm. Peace. Calm.

Become a silent observer of your slow, gentle, and easy breathing. Watch the breath as it comes in, and watch it as it silently leaves. Begin to notice the space between your breath that is still and silent. Peace. Calm. Peace. Calm.

Lean into that space between. In this moment, you can allow yourself to just fade into the distance. You can allow yourself to simply be. Peace. Calm.

Like an onion, you allow yourself to peel off your outer layer. Notice yourself become a little bit lighter, a little bit more free. Feel the peace. Feel the calm. Feel the space in between.

With every breath, you allow yourself to peel another layer. Witness yourself become more settled, more at ease, more peaceful and serene.

Notice how you can allow the gap to expand more fully as you peel away another layer with each and every breath. Peace. Calm. Peace. Calm.

Observe how it flows naturally and easily as you dip into this space that glows with truth, glows with purity, glows with You. It glows with peace and calm.

Allow yourself to be here in this space between, where there is nothing. And that nothing is everything that is true and authentic. That space of nothing is peace and calm and stillness.

Just be here, in the stillness, where all is well.

When you are ready, return your awareness to your surroundings. Take a deep breath and breath in peace; exhale calm; and be in that stillness.

And so it is.

TRUST

"*Trust in the Infinite Wisdom of the Universe*"

Many things in life can challenge you in ways in which you have no answers. You can try to comprehend the understandable, but often things are no clearer in the end than they were in the beginning. A shift into trust and acceptance can help you surrender to the infinite wisdom coordinating the necessary details that will enable the unfolding of your best and highest good.

So many families and people have dark shadows. You can allow your mistakes and learning choices to shift you out of the flow of the Universe. You can claim the wrong doings, mistakes, and poor choices of others as your own. You can limit yourself, your beliefs, your options for who you are, what you are capable of, and what and who you are to become. Through force or your own ignorance or inaction, you can allow others to decide your life for you. You can spend many years chasing the emptiness inside of yourself, wearing a false mask of your true self, while desperately seeking approval from everyone but yourself; believing that somewhere, something, or someone else will always be better, and that when you achieve that next thing, everything will be better and the world would make sense. You can become a shadow of your true self.

But no longer. You now know better. No longer will you hide. No longer will you run. No longer will you share the burden of the lessons for others, for it is theirs alone. No longer will you allow them or yourself to be your excuse. No longer will you compromise. No longer will you allow your past to dictate your future, for it is yours to claim. You will hold your head up high, trusting in the infinite of the wisdom, knowing everything is happening as it should and in perfect order.

You will claim the life you long to live. Now is the time for you to be all you can be. Today is the day you can decide that the things of your past will not cloud or dictate your present or future. Let them go. Free yourself from those heavy burdens you've carried far too long. Begin anew. Begin in this moment.

In this moment, you can choose your future. Choose peace. Choose joy. Choose forgiveness. Choose love. Choose to trust that the situations and people you encounter are holy encounters that are in and for your best interest.

This visualization exercise will allow you to reconnect to the deepest aspects of yourself to be reminded that you are a powerful being with tremendous gifts, talents, and abilities that are uniquely yours. You can move forward with the confidence in yourself and the choices you make for the best and highest good of yourself and those around you, as you begin to believe more fully in who you truly are.

VISUALIZATION - TRUST YOURSELF

*S*it comfortably. Take a deep breath and as you allow yourself to settle more deeply into a relaxed position, you can allow your body and mind to begin to become a little more peaceful and a little more relaxed. This time, here in this moment, is just for you. A time to connect to that calm and peaceful place that is always within you. So just allow your breath to become so very soft and gentle, flowing so very easily and effortlessly.

As your body and mind continue to become more relaxed and at ease with each passing breath, you can allow your mind to float and drift in a space of velvety darkness that wraps itself around you like the embrace of an old friend. And in that space of darkness, you may begin to see light or color or other things that will support you on your journey within.

There is a voice that whispers to you. You hear that voice clearly, and that voice says...You have all that you will ever need. The answers you seek will be revealed when you focus your attention inward.

You, and only you, know what is best for you. You know what you need. And as of today, you only accept into your life those things that are in your best interest. You seek only what is beneficial. And you know what is right ... you can feel what is right ... by looking within yourself.

You now trust your intuition. And as you rely upon the inner nudgings, the internal knowing, and gut feelings you have always experienced, you feel confident your decisions will lead you to where you need to be. You trust your intuition. And you are confident in your decisions.

And as of today, you only allow the opinions of others to have a positive influence upon you. You stand firm for what you believe in. You stand firm for what you believe is true. And although you may consider what others have to say ... in the end ... you know the decisions are yours to make. And you know you will make the decisions that are right for you.

And all thoughts, feelings, and behaviors reflect how powerful you truly are. You are very powerful. You have the ability to achieve everything you desire. Simply look inward and the answers will appear. You have the power to change your life. And as you focus your attention inward and trust yourself, you become aware of all of your possibilities.

You have the courage to follow your heart, and your dreams. And you feel the reward of any risks taken to achieve your goals.

You feel happy, proud, confident, and at peace, with yourself. You know you will get to where you are going. And you feel the power of each decision you make, as you trust yourself and look inward to find the answers.

WISDOM

"*I Trust the Wisdom that Brought Me Here*"

I've come full circle. I left my life. Literally fleeing from it, I settled as far away as deemed necessary from all the history and drama of my life up until that point.

The funny thing is that although I created a new life in which I was no longer aware of the daily familial happenings, the history and drama was still within me.

I did not know to not pack that baggage when I fled the first chance I felt strong enough. I did not know it would linger and poke its head out at all the wrong times and in all the wrong places. It was only after much inner work and healing that I was able to see more clearly. But even then it was still present.

By the grace of my daughter's birth, I began to see things differently. The things that I once fled were now some of the things I longed for. Deeply. I understood them in ways that I wasn't able to before.

By the grace of my father's death, I allowed much of the history and drama that I had carried to end that day before his passing. I so wish he could be with me now to feel my love in a way I was never able to welcome before. But now I do it for me.

It is a choice. A choice about how to live. A choice about how to love. A choice about how to let go. When it all falls down, you are left with only you and the choices you make; and the choices you make are influenced by your ability to gain the wisdom that each moment provides.

What will you choose to carry with you?

This visualization exercise will allow you to internalize the idea that all of life – the good and the bad – is a process of learning, and everything you encounter provides the opportunity to gain the necessary wisdom that will enable you to make the best possible choices moving forward.

VISUALIZATION - BUILDING BLOCKS

*T*ake a deep breath, and as you exhale, allow yourself to get a little more comfortable and a little more relaxed. Let go of any tension or tightness in your neck or shoulders, and notice the way your eyes feel right now. Allow your eyelids to get heavy, loose, and relaxed. Perhaps you'd like to close your eyes right now or maybe you would like to in a few moments when it feels just right for you... knowing there is nothing you need to do, nowhere for you to be, nobody is wanting anything from you, nobody is expecting anything from you.

So you can just allow yourself to perhaps become aware of the sounds around you, and you can allow those sounds to begin to relax you. Allow those sounds to float in and out of your awareness, and allow the muscles of your body to relax so deeply and completely, as you become more relaxed than you could possibly imagine.

Let your body breathe so very softly, gently. Notice that each breath effortlessly floats in and then out of your body, and every time you exhale you relax into those sounds around you, breathing so easily, softly, slowly. Anytime you'd like to

relax deeper, you take a breath, and as you exhale you go even deeper within into that perfect and peaceful place of home.

As you allow your body and mind to relax in this perfect and peaceful place, you know this is a place where you can go for wisdom, learning, and truth.

You understand that everything in your life has been stored in your innermost mind. Since your birth, all sights... all sounds... all thoughts... all feelings... all information you have ever received or understood has been saved... your subconscious has a record of your entire life. Nothing has ever been left out. And it has always been that way.

And since you were born, everything you have come into contact with has taught you something. Whether you were aware of it or not, does not matter... your subconscious has always paid attention. Either way, you have used all of these experiences as building blocks. And one by one, each has become the foundation of what you know and who you are.

And as you learn more and more... and are exposed to more and more... your building blocks continue to stack one upon another... upon another... upon another. There is no limit to how high and far you may reach. As you learn new skills, thoughts, and ideas... you increase your structure of knowledge. And every new building block not only serves to strengthen all of the previous blocks – the previous lessons – upon which it rests, but also to serve as the base for future lessons and future blocks to be placed upon. You already have a very solid foundation... and nothing can shake what you already know. You can never learn less, and never have fewer building blocks than you have already created. And this will never change.

You can only add more blocks... and more information... to the top of your stack. And the more you tend to your new block, the longer your new block stays in place, the more it becomes a part of you and your understanding. And the higher your stack climbs, the more quickly and more easily new building blocks stay in place.

With a belief in yourself comes a certainty that you are fully capable of accomplishing what you set out to do, and a sense of pride motivating you to achieve your goals. You must first believe in yourself before you can achieve anything.

As you use the building blocks of your past... of all that you have ever learned... you find it is easy to relate anything new you are faced with ... to a lesson you have already strengthened many times, in your growing foundation of knowledge. And as you recall your previous lessons to the current situation, the pieces of the problem seem to fit together more smoothly.

And if there is an area which is giving you some difficulty, you recognize the fact that you need additional explanation. As soon as you recognize this, you feel empowered... you know your own capabilities and understand the importance of allowing someone with more knowledge to guide you. There are no feelings of insecurity... and no feelings of self-doubt. To ask for help is to help yourself. There are instead, feelings of greater self-esteem and maturity.

And the questions presented are clear and easily under-stood. There is no confusion about the desired answer. And as you go along, the answers come into your mind without difficulty. The correct information easily appears in your mind's eye. And when you come to a question that requires more attention, you take a deep breath... and the answer reveals itself. And with each correct answer you provide, you become more confident... and more empowered... than you have ever been, as you realize you are achieving your goals. Through the hard work and dedication you have shown, you can see your structure of knowledge... your foundation... reaching and stretching farther than ever.

Feel yourself becoming so proud... so confident... and so

gratified, in all that you have accomplished... and all that you can accomplish in the years to come. And as you focus your attention on these feelings, you understand that if you allow yourself... your ever-expanding foundation will reach to limit-less possibilities if you first believe you can get there.

These words resonate deeply within your mind, body, and spirit. The core of your essence echoes the truth of this wisdom and you see, feel, and hear it in all parts of your being. And so you say to yourself...

My mind is open and receptive.
I release any past negative beliefs.
I let go of my negative past beliefs about myself.
I am willing to be intelligent.
I release my fears.
I embrace my wisdom.
I move past negative and limiting thoughts.
I deserve to be intelligent.
I give myself permission to be confident.
I give myself permission to succeed.
I give myself permission to expand my mind.
I give myself permission to be wise.
I give myself permission to forgive myself for things I wish to have been different.
I am grateful for all that I am, and all I have been through.
I am ready to learn and explore.
I am ready to discover my potential.
I am wonderfully wise.
Learning is easy.
I feel a new sense of curiosity when I am learning.
Intelligence is within me.
My mind grows with wisdom.
My mind vibrates with new information.
I can never learn less than I already know.

I increase my knowledge every day.

I feel my self-esteem rising each day.

My mind is like a sponge, easily absorbing and retaining information.

My mind is a powerful tool.

There is no limit to my potential.

My knowledge continues to grow every day.

My wisdom shines brightly.

Information is easily retrieved from my memory.

Nothing is ever lost in my memory bank.

I am confident in my abilities.

I know no boundaries.

My mind is always expanding.

As your subconscious mind and all levels of your inner mind are now memorizing this truth and awareness, you find it easy to incorporate all that you have learned into the fullness of your being... allowing this wisdom to influence your thoughts, feelings, and actions from this moment forward as you create your best life possible.

Take a nice deep breath in... bring your awareness back your surroundings... and open your eyes.

ABOUT THE AUTHOR

Krysti Turznik is an author, motivational speaker, and life coach. She holds a Masters Degree in Metaphysics, Bachelor of Science Degrees in Biology and Metaphysics, is an ordained minister, and a consulting hypnotist. For nearly two decades she's helped people get out of their own way and live the life they were meant to live.

Through mindset, motivation, and meditation she shows them how to create a life of miracles and magic where every day feels like a day at the beach. She lives in Wisconsin with her husband, daughter, and four cats.

For more information, as well audio recordings of the meditations from this book, please visit:

www.powerful-mind.com

www.ingramcontent.com/pod-product-compliance
Lightning Source LLC
LaVergne TN
LVHW011232080426
835509LV00005B/464